D0595540

REAL ESTATE PROSPECTING
THE ULTIMATE RESOURCE GUIDE

Loren K. Keim

ISBN 0-7414-4959-5

Published by:

INFIꝎITY
PUBLISHING.COM

1094 New DeHaven Street, Suite 100
West Conshohocken, PA 19428-2713
Info@buybooksontheweb.com
www.buybooksontheweb.com
Toll-free (877) BUY BOOK
Local Phone (610) 941-9999
Fax (610) 941-9959

Printed in the United States of America

Printed on Recycled Paper

Published November 2008

Acknowledgements

The 25 years I've spent as a Real Estate Agent and Broker have been an exciting adventure. The people who have helped me to perfect my prospecting programs are too numerous to mention, but I do want to thank some of the people who have significantly contributed to my programs (while hopefully not leaving anyone important out):

Theresa Keim, Tim Mahon, Ellie Barrett, Wayne Talaber, Mae Gunn, Judy Mazzeo, Marc Lucarelli, Joe Bartera, Pattie Hartman, Deb Hartman, Bonnie Smith, Kathy Reither Ziegler and many others!

I also want to thank the people who assisted me with editing and compiling all this information:

Betty Broadbent, Amanda Karpeuk, Keri Schlosser.

And, of course, this list wouldn't be complete without acknowledging some of the greatest real estate trainers in the country. I highly recommend anyone reading this book take the time to learn from each of these highly gifted trainers:

Floyd Wickman – www.FloydWickman.com
Joe Stumpf – www.byreferralonly.com
Dr. Dick McKenna – Co Creator of the Orbit Program
Ralph Williams – Co Creator of the Orbit Program

Table of Contents

Acknowledgements 1

Table of Contents 2

Chapter 1: Introduction to Prospecting 7
  What IS Prospecting? 10
  The Prospecting System: 12
  Selecting Your Target Market 12
  Selecting Your Method of Contact 15
  Giving Your Prospect Something of Value 19
  Follow Up Systems 20
  Summary 21

Chapter 2: Target Markets 23
  Start with Two 24
  Short Term Prospecting Markets 27
  Long Term Prospecting Markets 29
  Long Term Markets by Specific Type of Property 32
  Target Markets in Commercial Real Estate 33
  Passive Prospecting Sources 34
  Understanding Your Numbers – Short Term Prospecting
 34
  Understanding Your Numbers – Long Term Prospecting
 36
  Projecting Your Income 38

Chapter 3: Methods of Contact 41
  Methods of Personal Contact 41
    Door Knocking 42
    Workshops and Seminars 42
    Client Gatherings or Client Parties 43

Intentional Indirect Meetings 44
Booths at Events and Trade Shows 45
Methods of Phone Contact 46
Mailers 47
Letters VS Postcards 48
Emotional Response...50
Recipe Cards, Humorous Cards and Character Cards .52
Testimonials and Evidence of Success Mailings 53
Newsletters...53
E-mail...54
Special Delivery 54
Marketing...55
Summary 56

Chapter 4: Offering Something of Value............................59
Attraction Techniques 62
Newsworthy Marketing..64
Free Reports 65
Free Reports on the Internet..68
Market Evaluations 69
Automatic Listing Updates 70
Using a USP – Unique Selling Proposition 73
1 – Niche Market USP 74
2 – Unique Service USP..74
3 – Service or Performance Guarantee 75
4 – Comparison USP...76
USP Viral Marketing 76
New Listing Video 78
New Purchase Video 79
Summary 80

Chapter 5: Follow-Up Systems 81
Client Databases..82
Adding to your database 83
Drip Systems 84

Newsletters..85
E-Newsletters..86
Testimonial Letters..87
Evidence of Success Pieces...88
Mixing and Matching..90
Integrating Your Online and Offline Prospecting
Strategies...91
Humor 93
Promotional Items...95

Chapter 6: Initial Long Term Prospecting Methods 99
Sphere of Influence 100
    Creating Your Sphere of Influence List....................107
    Client Gatherings 111

Chapter 7: Short Term Prospecting Methods....................113
Cold Calling...114
    Elements of a Cold Call 115
    Cold Calling for Buyers 117
    Creative Cold Calling..118
    Voice Mail and Answering Machines.......................119
    Tracking your progress 120
Door Knocking...121
    Approaches to Door Knocking..................................122
    Door Hangers 125
    Three Step Door Knocking System...........................127
    Building your database..129
Vacant Lot Owners 130
Expired Listings Systems...131
    The Seller's Perspective..132
    Script for Calling Expired Listings 136
    Expired Listing System 1 – The Expired Package.....141
    Expired Listing System 2 – Morning Delivery..........143
    Expired Listing System 3 – Felt Tip Note Cards.......147

Expired Listing System 4 – Needle-in-a-Haystack
Boxes...150
Expired Listing System 5 – Crumpled Letters...........152
For Sale By Owners...154
The Reason 'For Sale By Owners' Fail.....................155
For Sale By Owner System 1: Relocation................158
For Sale By Owner System 2: I have a buyer...........164
For Sale By Owner System 3: Mortgage Co-
Conspirator..166
For Sale By Owner System 4: FSBO Survival Pack 168
For Sale By Owner System 5: The Honest Approach
....170
Other Short Term Prospecting Methods.......................172

Chapter 8: Other Long Term Prospecting Methods..........173
Farming for Business..173
A Farming Story...175
Farming Techniques..176
Pumpkins and Flags...177
Demographic Farming...179
Getting Around the Gate Keeper..............................179
Events and Sponsorships..182
Farming Office Complexes..183
Corporate Farming..185
Relocation Companies..186
Networking Organizations..187
Other Networking..188
Summary..189

Chapter 9: Using Guarantees..191
Lowering the Barrier of Resistance..............................192
The Listing Cancellation Guarantee.............................193
Call-Back Guarantee..195
Example:..197
Marketing Guarantees..197

Buyer's Guarantee – Sell it Free 198
Outrageous guarantees 199
We'll Buy Your Home – Fair Trade 201
We'll Buy Your Home – Outrageous Ad..................202
Cash Offer Guarantee..................................204
Buyers - We'll Buy Your Home Back 205
Summary 205

Chapter 10 – Putting it Together.............................207

Other Books by Loren Keim...............................213
Order online at www.RealEstatesNextLevel.com 213

Chapter 1: Introduction to Prospecting

In 1990, I stepped off a stage in Philadelphia after receiving an award for being one of the top producing agents in the State. A fellow agent from a competing firm sauntered up to me and snidely asked how *I* could possibly have sold so much Real Estate. I was 24 years old, but I looked like I was around 15.

The thought that went through my mind was that the reason I was successful was that I *had to* be. Financially, I was in deep trouble, and I simply had to sell a lot of properties or I would not only go under, but I would take down other people who I cared about with me. As the saying goes, necessity is the mother of invention. I became a top producer because I *had* to become a top producer.

Years later, I met an agent from Florida at a workshop who told a story of living in the attic of a barn and mucking out stalls for a living. She started selling real estate part-time in order to earn enough to get a decent apartment. A few years later, she was earning more than a million dollars a year in commissions.

Some of the top agents I've had the opportunity to meet with over the years have included people who started their careers while living on someone else's couch, or were the sons and daughters of immigrants with no background, connections or money when they first arrived in America. Yet, they became huge successes in the field of real estate.

Desperation is often the linchpin that drives us to those huge successes. I entered the real estate industry in the mid-1980s to help pay my way through college. By 1986 and 1987, the market was skyrocketing in the Northeast, and I started making a very good living simply sitting around waiting for the phone to ring.

In my incredible naivety, I thought the market was always like that. I could simply advertise a home, wait for the phone to ring and sell a few homes from the incoming calls. In 1988, my head had swelled up to roughly the size of a watermelon, because I was making more money than any of my friends and, therefore, thought that I was smarter than everybody else.

I talked my father, who at the time was a local school administrator, into buying into the local Century 21 franchise, and then into opening 3 branch offices in "growth" areas and finally into a land development. He mortgaged his house to the top of its value, and we borrowed other money at high interest rates. I wasn't worried, because I could always make more money, right?

1988 was the year of the great real estate crash in the Northeast. Property sales didn't simply slow down, they virtually stopped. My father had been looking forward to retirement, and we now owed nearly a million and a half with no substantial income to pay the payments. Although it's still a big sum today, in 1988, a million and a half was a huge sum of money. If something didn't happen quickly, he was going to lose his home and I'd be a large part of the reason because of irrational exuberance about the real estate field.

I was not someone who ever wanted to call a total stranger or knock on someone's door, but I also knew that I had to do whatever it took to find buyers and sellers. My father juggled numbers and credit, and I started calling expired listings, some for sale by owners, farming neighborhoods and sleeping very little. I wasn't really taking home much money because I was working simply to pay that huge debt.

We survived and came through the several year downturn in the market like a sling shot. At the time, however, I didn't think there'd be a day after tomorrow. I thought I was buried in a deep hole and would never see light again.

What really helped to save us, while many of our competitors closed their doors, was finding ways to capture a larger share of the real estate market and create business. There are always sales occurring in any market, good or bad. There are always buyers and sellers in the marketplace who want or need to buy. Some need to buy or sell because of job relocation needs. Others may have leases ending, a baby on the way, a pending divorce, a death in the family, or any number of reasons.

The key is identifying those people who truly want or need to move, and finding a way to meet with them. This concept of identifying and targeting likely buyers and sellers is called prospecting.

What IS Prospecting?

Many years ago, I found myself without a date for Valentine's Day. It was February 11th and I was in my mid-20's. I had recently broken up with a long-time girlfriend and wasn't sure what I wanted in a relationship. So I went to the local florist and ordered a dozen roses. I then asked the florist to send one rose to each of twelve different young women I had selected. The florist said *"You're kidding, right?"* I wasn't. That's called prospecting. Select a target audience and let them know you have something to offer them.

In the Real Estate Industry, as in most sales professions, prospecting is a dirty word. Far too many Realtors enter the field of Real Estate believing they can wait for the phone to ring and earn an above average income if they only select a brokerage with great advertising. Most new agents, as they venture into this endeavor, expect that the company will generate leads for them. While it is true that most good real estate organizations generate some buyers and sellers from the advertising done by the company, you will not make a great living at any company waiting for the phone to ring. That is the kiss of death in the real estate industry.

Prospecting, however, is not simply picking up the phone and calling possible buyers and sellers. To be effective, prospecting must be a consistent planned process. Your goal is to create a steady flow of business into your pipeline that will result in an above average income.

Your business will build like a wave over the long term of your career if you deliver exceptional service. Starting small, it can grow to tsunami proportions as more and more of your past clients, business associates, friends and relatives refer you business. It's a process to create those referrals, and you have to survive long enough in the industry, making a living, until you have a database of people who like and trust you that will continually feed and expand your business and client base.

There are two fundamental truths about prospecting.

The first truth is that you must prospect consistently to be successful. Set aside time each and every week to perform the task. If you don't block out time, other *stuff* will get in the way. *"Well, Loren, I couldn't prospect today because I* **really** *needed to go shopping for groceries, and I had an out-of-town client, and I had this awful hangnail."* My experience with training hundreds of Realtors over the years has taught me that prospecting is the hardest part of any real estate career. The number one reason that Realtors fail in this industry is that they fail to schedule the time to find prospects. This is particularly important early in a Realtor's career. In the long run, Realtors who deliver exceptional service receive many referrals from their clients, which limits the amount of prospecting successful Realtors need to do. However, when building a real estate business for yourself, you need to look at the various options available to seek out qualified property sellers and buyers.

The second truth is that prospecting is a *process,* not an *event.* Some real estate trainers teach Realtors to randomly pick up the phone and call people until they get an appointment. A much smarter approach is to carefully select a target market that you feel is not being serviced, or where you may find a competitive advantage, and lay out a game plan to target that audience. The game plan will include a method, or several methods, of contacting the target audience, a reason for your contact or something of value for the group you're prospecting, and a systematic way to follow up with that group.

The Prospecting System:

There are four steps to a successful prospecting system.

1. Select Your Target Market

2. Select Your Method of Contact

3. Give Your Prospect Something of Value

4. Follow Up Consistently

Selecting Your Target Market

When I opened my first real estate office in Allentown, Pennsylvania, I was competing with a huge company that advertised their firm was involved in 1 out of every 4 sales in my marketplace. There were many real estate companies and offices, but one stood out as the giant that we all had to compete against. This huge independent real estate firm, which we'll refer to as "M", had hundreds of agents, their own real estate television show and marketing brochures that I could only dream about.

So why bother competing? Partly because I didn't like the corporate feel of the large company, but mostly because I wanted complete control over my own transactions. I'm sure my ego figured in there a bit as well.

Since I was too small to compete head to head with such a behemoth, I dusted off my copy of the book *"Marketing Warfare"* by Reis and Trout, a book I highly recommend, and went to work on guerilla tactics for building market share. Reis and Trout explain that a small company should find niche markets. Clients like specialists, or someone who understands their particular market. A particular market can be a type of property, a particular area, or a combination of both.

We searched to find areas of real estate specialization that appeared to be ignored by the larger companies. The first target we selected was *Historic Homes*. Pennsylvania has plenty of stone Farmhouses, post-revolutionary brick Colonials, Victorian homes and many other unique dwellings with character. In order to attack this market, we began compiling a list of all the historic properties in the Lehigh Valley market area, where Allentown is located. At the time, we had to do this research from microfiche records because computer and Internet databases didn't yet exist.

In order to target this market, we started mailing letters asking them to call us if they were shopping for a "Historic Homes Specialist". The calls were few and far between. We decided to improve our message by giving the group something of value. We created a specific newsletter that we mailed to the group that had information on other historic homes, information on restoration techniques and other articles that owners of this type of property may find useful. We found that these newsletters had a much longer "shelf life" because the owners would hold onto them, and we received more calls from this group.

Next we started setting up free workshops that would be of value to our target group of historic home buyers and sellers.

I remembered attending a speech by the market guru, Jay Abraham, who explained that a salesperson can be perceived as an expert in a particular market or in a specific product by giving lectures or workshops.

We researched restoration projects and designed our free workshops to provide information on restoring historic homes. We provided tips to keep period character with modern functionality, and we even held seminars on financing these homes.

Finally, we sent announcements to the press explaining that we were the historic home specialists. The largest local newspaper, *The Morning Call*, ran a full page article about our team on the front page of the Real Estate section. Other magazines, such as *PowerSource*, also quoted us as the experts on historic property.

Although my team and I had learned a significant amount about historic homes, we had known very little when we first selected that audience as a target market. We had to research the marketplace and the needs and concerns of buyers, sellers and property owners in order to fully understand how to help them.

Our second target was equestrian properties. Like historic homes, we felt this group was not being specifically marketed. We researched the wants and needs of horse owners and created a marketing program that included advertising in equestrian magazines and a newsletter that went out to prospective horse farm buyers. As the World Wide Web came online, we created several websites that specifically targeted horse farm buyers and sellers. You'll find many of my articles on buying and selling farms all over the web today.

This program of targeting specific groups and creating a marketing program specifically designed to their needs was repeated with restaurants, liquor licenses, bank foreclosure departments, luxury properties, investment properties, corporate relocation departments and many other target groups. By the time we had completed our fifth or sixth target market, we had market share in virtually every part of our market area.

In Chapter 2, we'll outline many of the possible target markets and information on those markets. The important thing is to carefully select the group you plan to work with and build a business to the needs of the clients.

Selecting Your Method of Contact

There are literally hundreds of methods of contacting prospective buyers and sellers in your marketplace. Methods may include phone calls, door knocking, emailing, mailing, and some special deliveries. Some of them are quite fun, like delivering flags, pumpkins or hay boxes. We'll discuss these methods in detail in Chapter 6. All forms of prospecting, however, fall into 3 primary categories:

❑ **Hope For It** - Reactive Marketing or Prospecting includes advertising on shopping carts, park benches, in the newspaper or on the radio, and waiting in the office for the phone to ring so you can pick up a client. You will never become rich waiting for the phone to ring. You will be at the mercy of the market. Whether you're on floor time / opportunity time or specifically advertising for clients, it is unlikely that an agent will be successful by simply attracting clients through marketing. There are some methods we will outline in Chapter 4 to improve your odds, however.

❏ **Wait for It** – Proactive prospecting that is long term - Long Term Marketing is generally another passive form of seeking clients. Mailings, postcards, and similar methods generally produce very few immediate clients. Regularly mailing to organizations or individuals who are likely to buy, sell or expand in the future may bring business to an agent in the future. Joining referral or community organizations and promoting yourself regularly may bring future business as well.

❏ **Go Get It!** - Proactive Short Term Prospecting and Marketing – An agent who is actively seeking companies or individuals who need their assistance right now is proactively short term prospecting.

One of the great aspects of working in the Real Estate industry is that you can create your own business within a business, without the overhead of running your own company. This is an industry where you'll need inventory in order to survive. Your inventory is your portfolio of properties for sale or for lease. However, unlike most small businesses, you don't have to pay the carrying costs for purchasing inventory to sell. You are marketing someone else's product and being paid for that service.

In the beginning of your real estate career, unless you are independently wealthy, you're going to need to find clients who need to buy or sell right now. Finding clients who need to buy or sell right now is *"Proactive Short Term Prospecting"*. That might mean sitting down and calling every property owner along Rosebud Boulevard in your city or every owner in a particular neighborhood to find out if they're considering moving up to a larger home, moving down to a smaller home, or looking to buy an investment property or second home. It might mean stopping by every home in your own neighborhood to meet the owners and ask if they plan to move now or anytime in the near future.

You may call everyone advertising in the newspaper that they're trying to sell a home on their own, or call everyone who had their home on the market last year and were unsuccessful in selling. You may even try calling everyone in the wedding announcements section of the local paper to see if they're planning to purchase a home.

Knowing that you probably have to go out and make cold calls or knock on doors is a hard pill to swallow for most new agents. However, you won't have to do it forever. You are building your own personal business for the long haul. As you treat these clients with professionalism, honesty and give them 100%, they will refer you other buyers and sellers and your personal business will grow.

"But Loren," our new agents usually start, *"can't I just start mailing brochures and postcards and stuff to the owners of property in the area I want to target? Won't that work?"*

Our experience is that if you mail huge volumes of material out to prospective clients, you will get *some* prospects, but not a lot. Think of all the junk mail you get at your home. Many people open their mail directly over the garbage can so they can immediately dump anything that looks remotely like a sales piece.

Our return on blind mailers to people we don't already have a relationship with has been about $1/10^{th}$ of 1%. So if you mail to 1000 prospective clients, one might contact you, and

a contact doesn't mean they're going to use your service. As
with any marketing or advertising, if you mail consistently
over and over again to the same group, they will eventually
begin to recognize your name and services. That may take a
year to eighteen months to start generating any possible
business. Most new agents can't survive a year and a half
without income, and most new agents who use mailers give
up before it has time to begin working.

What I recommend to new agents as they begin their journey
into the world of real estate is that they select two target
markets and two prospecting methods their first month in the
business, and grow from those two methods. One of the
methods should be long term, and one should be short term.
The best long term method, I believe, is to start consistently
contacting your sphere of influence, and add a minimum of 5
to 10 people to your sphere of influence each week.

Your sphere of influence is that group of people that you
interact with on a regular basis, including your family,
friends and past co-workers. These are the people who
already like and trust you. The only challenge with first
going after your sphere of influence is that they are hesitant
to entrust their most valuable asset to someone new in the
business, even if they've known you since you were in
diapers. We lay out an entire game plan to convince this
group to use you in Chapter 6.

For short term prospecting, there are many methods that
we'll discuss over the next few chapters. My suggestion is
generally to start with either calling or knocking in
neighborhoods where your firm recently sold a home, or to
call through expired listings. Expired listings are those
properties that were on the market, but expired from the
market without selling. In many cases these sellers still want

their properties sold, but were unhappy with their prior agent. Prospecting around homes that were recently sold by the firm is another good method because the firm already has a track record in the neighborhood, and everyone likes to know what homes like theirs are selling for.

Giving Your Prospect Something of Value

Where many Realtors fall short in prospecting is failing to give something of value to the person they're contacting. Our goal when prospecting is not *just* to sell a property. Many agents have a difficult time understanding this concept, but the primary goal of prospecting is to identify a potential client. You want to entice a client to raise their hand and acknowledge that they may be in the market to buy or sell some time in the near future.

For example, a buyer in the marketplace may be interested in purchasing a 3 bedroom, 2 bath ranch-style home in a particular school district 5-6 months from now. If you advertise a 3 bedroom, 2 bath ranch in that school district to that buyer today, he or she may not react and call you because he or she is not yet ready or able to buy. What you want to find out is who is going to be buying or selling over the next few months or few years and direct all your future mailing and efforts at those individuals.

One method of enticing buyers and sellers to raise their hands and let you know that they *will* be in the market shortly is to give them something that they consider to be valuable. Usually that something is information. This type of marketing is called "Direct Response Marketing". The Realtor, in this case, builds an advertisement with an eye-catching headline that causes the reader to go beyond the headline and look at the offer. The body of the ad then creates a compelling offer for some information that the prospective buyer or seller simply *has* to have. These offers may be based around fear of loss, possibility of a gain, or strong curiosity about a subject.

A prospective home seller may not respond to *"Call for a Free Market Analysis"*, but may instead call for a free informational booklet *"The 22 Critical Steps to Selling Your Home in Any Market"*. There has to be something that tweaks the prospective client's interest and leads them to call you.

Likewise, a prospective home buyer may not respond to *"Call me to learn about Buyer's Agency"*, or *"Pre-qualify for a new home"*, but might respond to *"Free Informational Booklet on How to Avoid the 7 Deadliest Mistakes Made by Home Buyers that Cost Them Thousands of Dollars"*.

Chapter 4 will focus entirely on offering something of value and explaining your own unique value as a Realtor in a sea of other Realtors.

Follow Up Systems

Once you've identified prospective future clients, you'll need to begin building a relationship with them. In general, relationships are based on individuals liking and trusting one another. It is difficult to make someone like and trust you simply by mailing "stuff" to them. However, you can build a relationship that provides value to the prospective client. Continue to give the prospect good information in small increments and provide them with the opportunity to respond to the information or request more.

Additionally, humor can be part of any follow-up campaign. Humor may not make the potential client think of you as the best, most knowledgeable person in the industry, but may humanize you and help the client to like you.

A successful follow-up campaign uses a variety of techniques and contact methods. According to Dan Gooder, author of *Real Estate Rainmaker*, another excellent book, one of the most important aspects of any campaign is to consistently "drip" on prospective clients, and therefore keep yourself in front of them. A good campaign integrates an online and offline strategy.

Some of the contact methods of keeping in touch with these clients include email, postcards, newsletters, mailings, personal handwritten notes and phone calls. When creating a mailing piece to maintain contact with your database of prospective clients, you can include testimonial letters, short stories about particular transactions, more informational brochures, local area information and general newsletters, among others.

Specific follow-up systems will be explained in Chapter 5.

Summary

Arthur Brisbane was quoted as saying "*The dictionary is the only place where success comes before work.*" The number one reason people fail in real estate is that they don't begin a prospecting program when they first begin their career in real estate. Real Estate can be a high paying and very rewarding career, but it takes effort and hard work when you first start.

Make sure you're not one of the many failures in your chosen career. Take the time to lay out a game plan to attack the market and build a business for yourself.

The four steps to a successful prospecting plan include selecting one or more target markets, selecting your methods to contact those target markets, giving your prospects something of value, and following up consistently.

A career in real estate is not hard. I didn't say that it was easy. I said it's not hard. All the tools and techniques to make yourself a success are available to you. We can reach back to those great real estate agents who've gone before us and use their systems.

What you need to do is apply the knowledge you receive to become the success I *know* you can become. If you read any book about Realtors who eventually become multi-millionaires, you'll discover a group of people who include one that started by living above a barn, mucking out stalls. You'll find one who was living on the floor of the local high school gym because he couldn't afford an apartment. Some are the children of immigrant taxi drivers or painters. The truth is that it is not who you know or what you know when you enter the field of Real Estate, it's whether or not you apply yourself to your career.

As Stephen King said, *"Talent is cheaper than table salt. What separates the talented individual from the successful one is a lot of hard work."*

Chapter 2: Target Markets

Wayne Gretzky: "You miss 100% of the shots you don't take"

Whether you're beginning your career in Real Estate, or knuckling down to try to increase your income, you'll need to select a target market or a target audience for your message. Certainly, like mega-sized real estate companies, you could attempt the shotgun approach and blast information to anyone and everyone, hoping someone will listen.

If this is your plan, you'd be better opening the lid of your toilet and carefully flushing one hundred dollar bills down it, because at least your expectations will be more in alignment with the results you'll see from your expenditures.

Remember that you *are* your own real estate company. Your firm may have the largest or smallest market share in your local market, but your personal market share will determine your personal income.

Specialization is one way to overcome the competition. When you're sick, you look for a specialist and when you're selling a property, you want someone who understands your particular type of property or neighborhood and has a track record of success.

You may want to select your target markets based on your past experience. If you have past experience restoring homes, you may want to target the historic homes market. If you're an avid golfer, you may want to target golf course communities.

Certainly, you should select your target market or markets based on where you believe you can make money, but you should be sure to select groups that *you* would want to work with. Find out what that group or market wants and needs and how you can deliver it to them.

Start with Two

As you begin the adventure of a real estate career, my suggestion is always to select two target markets and lay out a game plan to attack each.

While there are some significant benefits to concentrating on one specific market and servicing *only* that market, there are several distinct advantages to beginning with two.

First, the market you initially select may not work as well as you hope. You may find stronger competition than expected. You may find a dip in the sales of that marketplace, or you may simply select a market that will be wonderful in the long run, but very difficult to obtain immediate business from.

Secondly, if done correctly, two target markets give you the flexibility of developing a long term target, while taking advantage of the income from a short term target.

Third, most real estate markets are cyclical. Even though properties sell in every part of the country in every market, there are ups and downs in the local housing market. Careful selection of two diverse target audiences may actually help you to keep your business consistent over time.

For example, I mentioned in the first chapter that I have a specialty or target market of horse farms and equestrian properties. This has been one of my best target markets because it is a market that is widely ignored by the average real estate company, and real estate firms tend to market these properties simply as homes, which often misses many potential buyers. For example, the majority of equestrian property buyers search for the *perfect* property within an hour of their work, while the average home buyer narrows their search to one or two school districts. The other benefit of the horse property market is that the property prices tend to be significantly higher than the average sales price of a property in the area.

The negative aspect of equestrian properties is that they tend to be strongly affected by real estate down cycles. The value of land follows the typical housing market and declines because builders tend to buy far less land in down cycles. These properties can also be negatively impacted by down cycles in the horse industry, such as slow downs in horse racing or horse sales.

To compensate for this, one of my target markets is bank foreclosure departments. In a recessionary market, while home sales decline, the number of foreclosures actually tends to rise. This technique of choosing counter-cyclical markets is called hedging.

In the case of starting or restarting your career, these two specialties may not be a good combination because both are long term methods of business acquisition. Each requires some research and specific knowledge, and a period of time to make yourself known to the group in order to attract business from that group.

Whenever you're considering a target group, I suggest investigating the marketplace to determine the competition you'll face, and to properly understand the particular type of property you plan to market. Again, you'll need to discover what the group or market needs and what challenges they face in the sale or purchase of their property. Then you'll need to determine how you can deliver it to them.

When investigating the equestrian property market, I spent a considerable amount of time "previewing" horse properties and asking questions about *why* certain properties are preferable to others. What does a buyer want in a barn? What is an arena and what benefit does it offer the buyer? How much land do you need for one horse? What about 2 horses, or 10? What are the zoning requirements of having large animals on a property? Where do buyers of horse properties shop to find the right property? Do they use homes magazines or horse enthusiast magazines?

Bank foreclosures, which may be handled by REO (Real Estate Owned) departments in banks or may be subcontracted out to specialized REO companies, are completely different. While understanding the product is critically important to the equestrian property, understanding the process of foreclosure and how lenders work is the most important aspect of working with bank foreclosures. In either case, I had to approach the situation from the view point of the potential client in order to adequately service the market.

Again, you should start by selecting two target markets. One should be a long term target, such as a geographic farm, a demographic group or simply your sphere of influence. The other should be a short term target. Calling through a neighborhood where your firm recently sold a home, listings that expired with competing brokers or 'for sale by owners' are all excellent short term, quick listing markets.

There are literally hundreds, if not thousands, of potential target markets or target audiences for your message. The list included with this text is just a sampling of some of the many great potential sources of income for your business. Over the next few sections, we'll discuss methods of attacking many of the following target markets.

Short Term Prospecting Markets

❑ **Expired Listings** – Homes that had been on the market recently with a competing Realtor, but failed to sell. Many of these home owners are still interested in selling their properties. Expired listings are generally a short term prospecting source. We'll go over 5 different methods of contacting these properties in Chapter 7.

❑ **For Sale by Owners** – Owners who want to save the commission or don't trust a Realtor to handle all the details properly. What they find, over time, is that shoppers of by owner properties are also looking for a discount, and most by owners can't access the primary marketing tools necessary to get top dollar for their homes. Many, if not most, *"FSBO's"* list their homes with a Realtor.

☐ **Just Listed / Open House Prospecting** – A recently listed home in a neighborhood leads to neighbors considering the value of their homes. *"If the Smith's can move to a bigger home, maybe we can too."* Calling or door knocking around a new listing can often lead to multiple listings in the same area. Calling or door knocking just before an Open House and inviting the neighbors to the open house may entice them to talk with you about their situation. Again, many agents simply mail out "Just Listed" cards. Direct contact by phone or in person will be far more likely to net you potential clients.

☐ **Just Sold Prospecting** – Anyone thinking of selling a home in a neighborhood will be more likely to speak to the agent who just sold a home nearby. Calling 50 or more homes around a home you recently sold is a great way to build your personal listing inventory.

☐ **Life Events** – Announcements in the newspaper let you know when someone is planning a wedding, had a new baby or passed away. Each of these life changing events leads to a change in housing needs. These groups may be carefully contacted to determine their motivation and needs.

☐ **Apartments / Renters / First Time Buyers** – Although there are lifelong tenants in every part of the country, the average renter in many places rents for less than 3 years. Direct contact with this group can net many prospective buyers who will be looking for a home very soon.

❏ **Absentee Owners** – Owners that do not live locally. These owners may have inherited a property from a relative, or may have held onto a property when they were relocated. These properties may be short term or long term, because many of them come on the market each year.

❏ **Pre-foreclosure Properties** – Across the country, you can search properties that are in foreclosure, but have not yet been foreclosed. In order to foreclose on a property, the lender must file paperwork in a local court. Once you determine who is in foreclosure, you can contact these owners and attempt to list the properties. Hopefully you can sell the property prior to the Sheriff sale.

Long Term Prospecting Markets

❏ **Sphere of Influence** – This is a key critical component to your success. Building your personal database of friends, relatives, associates and past clients is very often the largest part of any successful Realtor's income stream. Each person you know has many other friends and relatives who they may refer to you. I highly recommend this group as your first target market. You'll find a specific game plan for this market in Chapter 6.

❏ **Foreclosed Properties** - REO (Real Estate Owned) Departments at banks seek out hard working Realtors to sell the properties they take possession of. In many cases, these banks already have a primary agent and several secondary agents in your marketplace. Maintaining consistent contact may get you added to the list.

- **REO Companies** – Companies who manage foreclosed or REO properties for many banks also need Realtors to sell their properties.

- **Builders and New Construction** – Many builders have an agent, firm or team of agents they've worked with for many years. However, builders do make changes in their marketing strategy over time. Your consistent contact of this group may lead to a lot of business over time.

- **Vacant Land Parcels and Lots** – Some owners purchase land as an investment with no intention of building. Some owners purchase land to build their dream homes, and their plans sometimes change. Contact with this group can be a lucrative source of listings.

- **Investment Property Owners** – There are several types of investment property owners. One type is continually looking to add to their portfolio of properties. These investors may become a great source of consistent income as they buy more properties. The second type is made up of owners of investment property that find it to be more of a hassle than they originally bargained for to own and manage real estate. These can be lucrative sources of listings as well. Additionally, like working with builders or REO departments, you may obtain many listings or sales from one single investor.

- **Geographic Groups** – Farming for clients has long been a staple of the real estate industry. This entails selecting a target area, such as a neighborhood, and contacting the area over and over again until you become known as the local neighborhood expert.

❑ **Demographic Groups** – Similar to geographic farming, a demographic group is a group of people in the same industry or with the same likes. You may specialize in working with doctors or attorneys. You may specialize in clients who are Veterans of a war or any other group. Some popular demographic groups include newlyweds, seniors planning retirement or empty nesters, and young families.

❑ **Third Party Relocation Companies** – Millions of employees are relocated around the globe each year. Some companies, like Cartus and Prudential, buy homes for employees being relocated by large companies. Other relocations companies, like Internation Relo, simply help manage the move. The fees to work in this arena can be very high, but the leads tend to be very good. If you're interested in corporate relocation, consider joining the ERC (Employee Relocation Council) and begin learning all you can about corporate relocation.

❑ **Personnel Departments** – The personnel director or human resources director knows who is being relocated into or out of the area. For small or medium sized companies with several offices, you may be able to offer relocation assistance.

❑ **Attorney Referrals** – Attorneys can be a wealth of listing, buying and investing opportunities for Realtors. Estate attorneys often handle the disposition of property for a deceased person's estate. Divorce attorneys and bankruptcy attorneys often refer agents when clients must sell property to finalize a divorce or bankruptcy.

Other attorneys refer agents when a client must sell a property in order to pay a settlement on a lost court case. Attorneys may be lucrative sources of business.

Long Term Markets by Specific Type of Property

☐ **Equestrian / Horse Property** - Animal friendly properties are a large target market in many parts of the country. Customers are looking for a place to call home for themselves and their horses, alpacas, or some other large animals.

☐ **Historic Homes** – Farmhouses, Victorian Homes, Tudor Homes, Log Homes, Homes with Character are all part of the historic home property type. Buyers of this type of property often purchase the property due to their love of the history, the character or thoughts of a simpler time.

☐ **Green Homes / Healthy Homes / Natural Homes** – One of the fastest growing market segments. Consumers are more conscious of their health and want to make sure their homes are health-friendly. Specialty builders across the country are beginning to look at this growing target market.

☐ **Contemporary Homes** – While some buyers look for homes with the character of an earlier era, other buyers are actively looking for the unique, the dramatic and the contemporary in their living accommodations.

☐ **Senior Communities** – Although this can also be considered a Demographic Group, senior communities of one level town homes, singles and condos are becoming more and more popular across the United States and around the world. Understanding the market for these can help you to build a strong long term business because seniors know other seniors who are also considering this lifestyle.

❑ **Special Location Homes** – Some agents specialize in golf course homes (homes on golf courses). Other agents study and understand the nuances of waterfront property. Special locations can include mountain top homes, view lots, beach front, lake front, park front or nearly any other premium location.

Target Markets in Commercial Real Estate

❑ **Office Buildings** – Some buyers purchase office buildings to lease them and receive a return on their investment, and others purchase them to use for their businesses.

❑ **Retail Properties** – These may also be purchased either for investment or for use in a business.

❑ **Industrial or Warehouse Properties** – These may also be purchased either for investment or for use in a business.

❑ **Hospitality Properties** – Hotels, Motels, Golf Courses and more.

❑ **Redevelopment Opportunities** – Some Realtors have made significant incomes identifying properties that are not currently at their highest and best use, and selling these properties to investors or investment pools to rezone or redevelop.

❑ **Business Brokerage** – Selling businesses is a specialty all its own. Business brokerage can be a very lucrative business once you understand all the nuances of financing, marketing and selling them because very few Realtors concentrate in this market.

Passive Prospecting Sources

❑ **Internet Leads from Re-Sellers** - Homegain, Lending Tree, RealEstate.com and many other Internet companies aggregate leads from potential buyers and sellers and sell those leads to Realtors and mortgage originators. These can be very expensive prospects and I've found that a plurality of them tend to be very poor.

Understanding Your Numbers – Short Term Prospecting

When attempting to determine what you need to do in order to earn the living you desire, you must first start by determining how many leads you need to generate into your pipeline, and how many will actually close.

When you're first starting out, you'll need to simply guess how many contacts you'll have to make in order to get a lead. Then you'll have to guess how many leads you'll need to capture in order to obtain a listing or a sale. Your manager, broker or trainer should be able to help you with these initial guesses.

As you begin working your prospecting strategy, you should track your results to determine your averages. For example, if you're consistently calling expired listings, you'll be able to calculate how many calls you make and how many appointments you realize out of those calls. There will be good days and bad days, but overall, you should find an average. Additionally, this will allow you to *test* different approaches, dialogues and strategies to improve your ratios.

If you're calling around neighborhoods where someone in your firm recently sold a home, you'll find some neighborhoods with a higher turnover may result in more leads, and some neighborhoods with a low turnover may result in fewer leads. Again, you can average how many contacts you need to make in order to earn your targeted income.

For example, in the chart below, the agent needs to attain one listing per week in order to attain their desired income level. The agent has determined that they will target the short term prospecting sources of "for sale by owners". The agent has further determined that they will obtain an appointment for every 20 calls they make to "for sale by owners" and will list one out of every three appointments they go on.

If this number of potential FSBO's is too large for your market area, you may need to select a second short term prospecting method.

Short Term Prospecting Needs

1. Number of listings needed per week: _1_ .

2. Number of appointments needed per listing: _3_ .

3. Average number of calls to get an appointment: _20_ .

4. Number of calls to make to FSBO's each week: _60_ .

Understanding Your Numbers – Long Term Prospecting

In order to effectively select a target, try to determine how much business may come out of that market. For example, if you're selecting a geographic farm, use the MLS or the local tax records to determine how many homes were sold in the neighborhood over the prior 12 month period.

If last year was a very strong year in the market, you may want to guestimate that the average year is a bit less. If last year was a very weak year for the local housing market, you may want to guestimate that a typical market is a bit higher.

If you have access to the records for the last 3 to 5 years, you may even want to research how many sales occurred in the area during those years in order to get a better handle on the yearly average. This research can also lead you to know whether or not there is already a competitor concentrating on this market. If one agent has a significant share of the listings and sales, that agent is probably working that geographic area.

Once you've determined how many homes you expect will be sold in your expected target market, you must realize that you may not make inroads into a long term market for more than a year, but you want an understanding of roughly how many homes sell each year.

You also need to understand that as hard as you might target a particular market, you will never get the entire market. Some home sellers will already have a relationship with an agent, or be related to an agent, or simply not like you or your firm. After 12 to 18 months of consistent contact, you should begin to receive a steady supply of contacts from the group. Within 24 to 36 months of consistent contact, you can achieve a market share of 25-50% of the homes in that market. The consistent contact needs to include some personal contact. An outline will be developed in Chapter 6.

You may find that your target neighborhood of 300 homes has a turn-over of one home for every six per year, or 50 sales per year. If you can achieve a 25-50% market share, that would equate to between 12 and 25 home sales from this one source.

If your long term prospecting source will not generate enough business for you, you may need to increase the size of your farm area. Also keep in mind that, as you deliver great service to these clients, they will also refer you business, multiplying your efforts over time.

Long Term Prospecting Needs

1. Number of homes / clients in market area: __300__ .

2. Number of listings per year in area: __50__ .

3. Percentage of likely customers to list: __30%__ .

4. Likely number of listings from this source: __15__ .

If your target market is not a specific area, you may have to take an educated guess on how many sales are generated in your target group, and what ratio you'll be able to achieve.

Projecting Your Income

Ultimately, you need to determine how large a target group you must select in order to achieve your income goals. Your broker, manager or trainer may be able to help you with determining how many people you must contact.

When I'm calculating a possible income, I also base it primarily on listings sold. It's far too difficult to predict when a buyer might show up and buy a home.

Projected Income

1. Desired Income = $100,000 .

2. Average Sales Price in Market = $200,000 .

3. Average Commission Rate in Market = 2.75% .

4. Average Office Income Per Transaction = $5500 .
   (Avg Sales Price * Avg Commission)

5. Your Average Commission Per Transaction = $3850 .
   (Avg Office Income * Your Commission Split)

6. Number of Sales Needed Per Year = 26 .
   (Desired Income / Your Average Commission)

7. Percentage of Listings taken that Sell = 70% .

8. Number of Listings Needed Per Year to Generate Number of Sales Required (26 / 70%) = 37

9. Number of Appointments to generate 1 listing = 3 .

10. Number of Appointments needed = (37 * 3) = 111 .

11. Average Number of Calls / Contacts to obtain an appointment = 60 .

12. Total Number of Calls / Contacts necessary = 6,660.

13. Number of Calls / Contacts to make per week = (6660 / 52) = 128 .

Projected Income

1. Desired Income = _____.

2. Average Sales Price in Market = _____.

3. Average Commission Rate in Market = _____.

4. Average Office Income Per Transaction = _____.
   (Avg Sales Price * Avg Commission)

5. Your Average Commission Per Transaction = _____.
   (Avg Office Income * Your Commission Split)

6. Number of Sales Needed Per Year = _____.
   (Desired Income / Your Average Commission)

7. Percentage of Listings taken that Sell = _____.

8. Number of Listings Needed Per Year to Generate Number of Sales Required (___ / ___) = _____.

9. Number of Appointments to generate 1 listing = ___.

10. Number of Appointments needed = (___ * ___) = ____.

11. Average Number of Calls / Contacts to obtain an appointment = ____.

12. Total Number of Calls / Contacts necessary = _____

13. Number of Calls / Contacts to make per week = (___ / ___) = ____.

Chapter 3: Methods of Contact

Christopher Reeves: *"Either you decide to stay in the shallow end of the pool or you go out in the ocean."*

George Eliot: *"It's never too late to be who you might have been."*

Once you've decided on your target markets, you'll need to devise a plan to contact those markets and show those markets the value of your services. Some methods of contact are direct contact, such as calling or mailing to a specific person. Some methods of contact are simply marketing, such as putting your message on a park bench or bus stop or running a gigantic ad in the yellow pages.

Direct contact falls into five major categories: by phone, in person, by mail, by email or special delivery.

Methods of Personal Contact

Personal contact doesn't simply mean knocking on the door. Any time you can get a prospective client to meet with you in person is a personal contact. Some methods include:

Door Knocking

The most dreaded of all contacts, but often the most effective. There is nothing better than personal contact to build a relationship with a potential client. Door knocking can be a long term prospecting method, when done in a geographic farming area. Door knocking can also be a short term prospecting method when done around recently sold listings, or to invite neighbors to an Open House.

In Chapter 8, we'll introduce you to people earning over a million a year from door knocking.

Workshops and Seminars

Another great source of business can be created by marketing yourself as the local expert in some niche market. One of the best ways to set yourself apart as the expert is to hold workshops on subjects that would interest your target audience. While hosting a workshop, you are immediately seen as the expert in the field.

For example, if you're already mailing to everyone who owns a historic home, invite them to a free workshop on restoration projects. When holding the workshop, include a three minute presentation on why you are the best person to help them market their property.

If you're concentrating specifically on selling investment properties, you may want to target doctor's groups, attorneys and other possible investors. Contact the local hospitals to set up a workshop in the hospital for the employees on *"How to invest in Real Estate"*, *"How to leverage your assets to increase your investment portfolio"* or *"How to find great tenants for your investment properties."*

An agent in our firm found a lucrative source of business by partnering with local independent living and assisted living facilities. He offered free seminars to prospects of the facility on how to sell your home for the most money possible and make the transition into elder care as painless as possible. This workshop was sponsored by the facilities, including the cost of the mailings. Even better, the facilities he has worked with actually provided the mailing list of their potential clients. This was a true win-win for both the agent and the facility.

Client Gatherings or Client Parties

A client gathering, like a seminar or workshop, puts you at the center of attention. You are the planner and organizer and the one who makes contact to set up the gathering. There are several ways to hold client gatherings or client parties.

The first kind is a party to benefit a particular client. For example, on many occasions members of my team would set up a *"meet your new neighbor"* party for a buyer moving into an unfamiliar neighborhood. The agent would contact all the surrounding properties and invite them to a party to welcome your buyer into their neighborhood. This benefits you, as the agent, in several ways. You certainly make an impression on your client, often leading to an unending stream of referrals from that client. Additionally, you get to meet many of the neighbors, who now know that *you* are the person who sold the home, which makes you the person to talk to when they decide to sell.

The second kind of gathering is a party for your past and current clients. Most successful real estate professionals I've met over the years have held annual client events, whether the events are small cocktail parties, summer picnics, movie nights or big events.

When you invite your clients to a gathering, you are inviting them into the inner sphere of your life and seeing them on a more social level. This makes them far more willing to refer you to their own friends and relatives. The other benefit of client parties is that you become the center of attention. The only thing your guests have in common is you.

Cocktail parties and summer picnics are always an easy party to plan and execute. More creative gatherings include inviting a sampling of your best clients to the opening night of a movie, at your cost. You may even be able to work out a discount for tickets ahead of time if you purchase enough. Perhaps you can do an evening at a sporting event or a cultural event. You are only limited by your imagination.

Intentional Indirect Meetings

There are many ways to facilitate your clients introducing you to other prospective clients. One of our favorite methods is to stop by a client's workplace with good news. For example, a buyer may *know* that they will be approved for their mortgage, but deep down in their gut, they're still worried about the outcome. Ask your mortgage officer *not* to call the buyer with an approval. Instead, let you know when the mortgage is formally approved so you can take the news directly to the buyer at their place of employment.

Stop by the local grocery store and pick up a half dozen helium balloons and a card of congratulations. This may cost you three or four dollars. Then bring the balloons and card with you and surprise the client. In my experience, the client is always happy and relieved. This buyer is likely to walk you around their office and introduce you to everyone. *"Hey, this is* **my** *Realtor. He is the best."*

Booths at Events and Trade Shows

Although I honestly have not found this to be a very effective tool, there are Realtors around the country who swear by event marketing. Simply put, event marketing is setting up a booth at a show for the market you plan to target.

Some Realtors use trade shows and events as their entire marketing program, going from senior living show to senior living show. I suggest, however, you make this method of contact a part of any target marketing you do.

For example, if you are targeting the horse farm market, there are plenty of horse shows throughout the country. If you plan to target the demographic group of empty nesters, you may want to set up shop at elder care shows or senior events. Most metropolitan areas have some form of a *"Seniorfest"*.

Another common type of show is home building shows, where you can target either builders or buyers of new construction, or home remodeling shows where you can still target home builders or those who decide remodeling is too big a project.

Other shows include wedding planning shows, first time home buyer shows, investor and estate planning shows, and many others.

Methods of Phone Contact

The phone can be used for many different purposes: following up with clients, prospecting neighborhoods where you know no one, or prospecting neighborhoods where you've already been farming. Please keep in mind that you have to cross index each call against the do-not-call list, and remember that not *every* phone number is part of that list. There are still many people you can call.

There are several different reasons you can call. A simple straightforward call to see if they're interested in selling is often the best approach. When calling, always try to identify the party first.

Agent: *"Mrs. Smith?"*

Client: *"Yes?"*

Agent: *"Hi, this is Albert calling from On Call Realty. I'm sorry to bother you at home, but we're selling a lot of homes in the neighborhood and I was just wondering if you'd be interested in selling your home?"*

Another approach is to give the potential customer information:

Agent: *"Mrs. Potter?"*

Client: *"Yes?"*

Agent: *"Hi, this is Cedric calling from Dumbledore Real Estate. I'm sorry to bother you at home, but we've just sold your neighbor's home – the Grangers at 5755 Privet Drive. We had a lot of interest in the home. It's much larger than it appears from the outside, and we're trying to find anyone else in the neighborhood who is considering selling. Do you know anyone planning to make a move?"*

Client: *"I knew the Grangers. How much did the home sell for?"*

If the potential client asked for the sales price, they may be considering selling themselves. Follow up with a hand written note after speaking with them.

A less aggressive method of phone contact might be to simply call as a public service. You can call just before elections and remind them to vote. *"Hi, this is Ralph Loren calling from Polo Realty. I'm just calling to remind you to vote in tomorrow's primary. Every vote counts, and if you plan to sell your property in the near future, please remember us at Polo Realty."*

You may call to remind them that they need to replace their smoke alarm batteries twice a year, or that the local community park is having an event or any number of other public service calls.

The important thing to remember is that phone calls are far more effective and more personal than mailing a letter or postcard.

Mailers

As I mentioned earlier in this text, our return on blind mailers to people we don't already have a relationship with has been about 1/10th of 1%. Mailing to 1000 people may generate only one single lead which may or may not turn into a client.

Mailers can be effective in three circumstances.

1. **Mailing to people who already know you** – your sphere of influence and past clients are 3-4 times more likely to read your mail than clients who do not know you. This type of communication is used to remind them that you're out there and hoping for their referrals.

2. **Mailing to the same group of people over and over again** – Farming by mail takes a long time to generate any response, but over time you will find that people will begin to remember you. This is a costly and difficult method of business development.

3. **Mailing value-added pieces with strong headlines that evoke an emotional response** – as you stand in a check out line at a grocery store, your eyes are naturally drawn to the cover of a tabloid featuring a baby with 3 heads. A shocking headline can often cause someone to open or read your letter. Offering a free report or something of value may get a client to respond to your letter. This will be further developed in Chapter 4.

Letters VS Postcards

Letters allow you to send lots of information in the same envelope to a prospective client. Letters can be effective if they are hand addressed and physical stamps are stuck to them. If the letters are printed from a program with a bulk rate stamp on them, they are less likely to be opened because the receiver already knows it's an advertisement.

However, if you are mailing to hundreds or thousands of potential customers, it is very difficult to hand address the letters. Some agents overcome this problem by putting special teasers on the outside of the envelope. *"Learn the 9 Powerful Secrets of Selling Your Home for Top Dollar Inside!"*

Postcards are more likely to be read because the receiver doesn't have to physically open them. Postcards don't allow a lot of room for information, but that might be beneficial because you'll have to narrow your focus down to the most important point. Determine what your unique strength or strategy is and put it on the card.

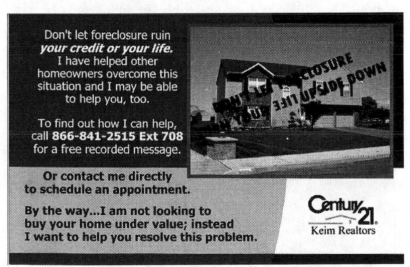

Postcard targeted at home owners in foreclosure.

Emotional Response

Whether you're sending a postcard or a letter, your goal is to get the recipient to read your message and hopefully take action. The action you desire is for that potential client to pick up the phone and call you with a need.

A strong headline is more than half the battle in getting your message read by the recipient. People read grocery store tabloids because they're sucked in by the headlines. The same methods can be applied to real estate letters and postcards.

For example, most Realtors put *"Just Listed"* or *"Just Sold"* on postcards. Not only are those dull and uninteresting headlines, but they are done in Realtor-lingo instead of plain English. Try having a little fun with your postcards. One of our agents sends out postcards like this:

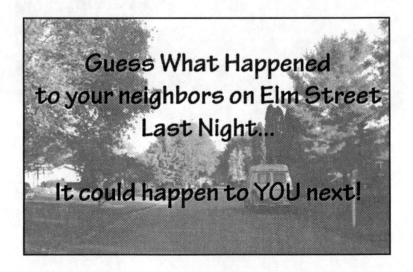

Is this card more likely to be read than the typical "*Just Sold*" card? Your goal in writing anything to a potential client is to get them to read your message. A strong headline helps to accomplish that task. On the reverse side of the postcard, you can explain that their neighbors sold their home for a great price in a reasonable period of time because they hired you as their experienced professional. If anyone else would like their home sold quickly, they can call you. Another closing to the back of the card might be to offer free information over the phone of what homes in the area are selling for.

Another of our agents used this card:

> # Your Neighbors,
> # John & Sally Smith
> # Got EXACTLY
> # What They Deserved...
>
> # And YOU Could Be Next!

The reverse side states that the neighbors sold their home for a great price, which is exactly what they deserved. If the reader is interested in the same kind of exceptional service, they can certainly call you for a free market analysis to determine their property's highest and best price.

Recipe Cards, Humorous Cards and Character Cards

Yes, it's true that some people really do take your recipe cards and file them in a 4" x 6" card holder to use in the future. However, the majority of them throw them directly in the trash. Another problem is that most of the people who see these cards don't associate them with you because recipes have nothing to do with real estate.

Does that mean it's a bad idea to send recipe cards? Not necessarily. Your goal is to communicate with your database of potential clients. If you happen to be part of a cooking club or you're farming restaurant owners and chefs, recipe cards may be appropriate. For most clients, however, you can probably find a better message to send.

The same applies for character cards and humorous cards. People love Mickey Mouse, Batman and Tinker Bell, but will it make them call you to buy or sell a home?

Don't misunderstand me, I sent out thousands and thousands of humorous cards over my career. For example, like many other agents, I sent out a postcard with the words "*Loren Keim is outstanding in his field.*" The postcard featured a photo of me standing in the middle of a field. There are people who can recall some of my more creative postcards and messages years after I send them. Unfortunately, that doesn't give the prospect the desire to pick up the phone and call me; it simply builds an image in their mind.

Testimonials and Evidence of Success Mailings

A more effective method of communication is to give the prospect something that shows them the value of working with you and makes them a compelling offer. We'll be discussing offers in detail in Chapter 4.

Testimonial cards or letters are simply stories written about you by one of your clients. This third party endorsement of your services can be very powerful. A strong headline might read "*My Realtor Saved My Marriage*". The body of the article might show how the husband and wife were arguing because their home wasn't selling. They switched agents and hired you, and you sold the home quickly, helping to restore the sanctity of their home.

Perhaps a more realistic one is "*My Realtor Helped Me to Buy a Home with No Money Down*". If you're targeting renters, they may be enticed to read through the article. "*Fantastic New Government Loan Program Helps Buyers Purchase Homes With Little or No Down Payment*" is another strong headline.

Even if you're simply sending a "*I Just Sold Your Neighbor's Home*" card, you're still showing some evidence of your success as a Realtor. A more effective method is to give a more shocking headline that will cause the recipient to read the rest, and turn that card or letter into a story about the transaction. Figure out what problems you had in that transaction and how you solved them.

Newsletters

As with any mailer, a newsletter will be read by some recipients. In order to maximize the number of readers, make sure to include emotional headlines and strong material that includes evidence of your success as a real estate professional and a reason for the prospect to call. Offer a free booklet, free informational pamphlet or other offer.

Personalizing newsletters can help as well, but are most effective when you're mailing to people who already know you. Several of our agents include stories of their kids in their newsletters. This generally will only be read if the reader is already familiar with you, such as a past client or a member of your sphere of influence.

E-mail

Nearly any message you can mail can also be emailed. You can even attach audio and video to your email messages. The benefit of email is that it is free to email most messages to your clients or prospective clients. The negative side is that email is often deleted without ever being opened.

As with any mailing piece, you must be certain to include a strong headline that will evoke an emotional response or at least a curiosity that will lead to the recipient opening and reading your message.

Special Delivery

Tom Hopkins is well known as one of the fathers of modern real estate salesmanship. His books and video training are worldwide best sellers. One of the acts he is well known for is delivering pumpkins to his geographic farm area during the Halloween season. We refer to that act as a Special

Delivery because it's not quite a mailing and it's not simply meeting your prospective clients.

Marketing

Most image marketing is not direct contact. You're simply putting your name and image out in the public trying to evoke a response or draw people in to call you. While most generic image advertising or image marketing truly *is* the "shotgun" approach to real estate, you can use *attraction techniques* to improve your odds of actually making the phone ring.

The problem with most image marketing is that it markets *you* or your company instead of marketing what the client wants. Clients respond to what is interesting to them. While all those wonderful billboards with Realtor's faces on them might make you recognizable, and may make you feel good, it is unlikely that they will produce any verifiable results. The only real benefit to straight image advertising is that it reminds your sphere of influence and past clients that you are in the industry, and makes you more recognizable when you get an appointment. It generally does not make people call you, and honestly, a lead is what you're trying to generate.

"Attraction Techniques" or Direct Response Marketing is the art of using a strong headline, followed by an offer to the potential client of something of value or of something that is of interest to the potential client. We'll be discussing how to build these techniques into all your marketing pieces in the next chapter.

There are almost limitless places to put your message. For example, marketing sources include:

❏ Signs, banners or your personal message on your car. ❏ Radio Advertising ❏ Television Advertising ❏ Newspaper Advertising ❏ Homes Magazine Generic Ads ❏ Magazine Advertising ❏ Billboard Advertising ❏ Shopping Cart Ads ❏ Yellow Page Ads	❏ Moving Van Ads ❏ Park Bench Ads ❏ Specialty Items / Give-a-ways ❏ Internet Banners ❏ Web Site Links ❏ Back of Grocery Store Receipts ❏ Local Sport Team Shirts ❏ Many, many other ways!

Summary

Prospecting is the art of making contact with potential buyers and sellers in the marketplace in order to deliver your message and hopefully entice clients to work with you. These potential buyers and sellers can be contacted in many ways, using a variety of methods.

You can either try to attract these potential clients through your marketing, which tends to be the least effective method, or directly contact these clients by selecting a target market and continually contacting the group.

Direct contact methods include contact by mail, by phone, in person, by email or by special delivery. If mailing or emailing to a target group, you should always include a consistent, easy-to-remember message and give the reader a reason to call.

Meeting clients in person can be done in many effective ways, including door knocking, workshops or seminars, client gatherings or parties, and intentional indirect meetings, among others.

If you attempt to call clients, you should have a concise, direct message that offers a benefit to the person you are calling.

Chapter 4: Offering Something of Value

Emmitt Smith: "A Better tomorrow takes your best today"

In the early 1990's, I met a gentleman at a Ron Rush workshop named Gerry Ballinger. Gerry, I believe, had been in management with Long & Foster in Virginia. He argued with a group of us that most Realtors create marketing messages that sell the agent, instead of attracting the customer.

Steve Furst is First in Real Estate!

Alex is Number One in San Diego Sales!

Be Sold on Sally!

*You can't go wrong with the Wright Team,
Call Bill and Ally Wright!*

Carla Castles – Your Source for Buying your Castle!

Ed & Danny - Simply the Best in Service!

In order to keep from being sued by someone somewhere named Steve Furst or Carla Castles, please understand that these names are fictitious and should not be construed as having any relationship to any person, living or dead.

The problem with all of these ads is that they really don't say anything. They have catchy phrases that a customer may remember but they don't give any reason for a potential client to take action. It is highly unlikely a buyer will pick up the phone and call Sally, because they want to be "*Sold on Sally!*"

There is a much better way to attract clients and entice them to raise their hands and let you know they're in the market to buy or sell. That method is by offering the customer something of value, or a fair trade that lowers the barrier of resistance a client has for calling you.

Something of value may be a free report or guide that will help their specific situation. It may be an offer of an over-the-phone evaluation of their property or situation, or a special tool such as an automatic listing update program.

This technique, as introduced to me by Gerry Ballinger, is known as Direct Response Marketing. Since that workshop, I've seen very similar materials from great trainers like Joe Stumpf[1], Terry Hunefeld, Jay Abraham, and Craig Proctor. Each uses a "direct response" mechanism in their marketing to get clients to identify themselves *as* clients or to lower the barrier of resistance in speaking with you.

---

[1] Joe Stumpf is the creator of The Main Event real estate training program and has developed a system of building business by referral. His training events are listed online at www.byreferralonly.com.

In many cases, top trainers like these suggest that you create advertisements that look like news articles. Consumers don't like *"sales people"* trying to *"sell them"* something. When they see advertisements that are sales-like, they put up their defenses. The potential customer believes that something must be untrue or hidden in the advertisement. In fact, many consumers will actively avoid speaking with an agent who uses the phrase *"Be Sold On ..."* because they believe they themselves will be *sold*.

Everyone likes to buy, but no one likes to be sold. This technique of creating articles that give away free information to the consumer allows the agent to "fly under the radar" of the consumer's defense mechanism. If consumers can view you as a valuable partner in the process of buying or selling, rather than a salesperson, you are most of the way to extraordinary success in your chosen field.

Unfortunately, this technique is so far outside the scope of most real estate agents and brokers thinking that they actively argue with me when I teach it. *"No one is going to call for some pamphlet. If we want buyers, we need to advertise homes."* I can tell you from experience that I have received significantly more calls on correctly structured newsworthy ads than I have from any advertisement on a particular home.

As I write about these techniques, please don't misunderstand, there are places and times for image advertising. For many years, I've used sign riders that read *"Keim Sold Mine!"* When you are trying to actively build name recognition, cute ads may get you noticed, but they will not make the phone ring.

Attraction Techniques

Understanding how to attract prospective buyers, sellers and investors to call you is both a science and an art form. You must start by considering what the prospective client desires and needs, and just as important, what they will actively avoid. Think from their perspective.

For example, in most cases, buyers do not really want to talk to us. They are afraid of being sold, or of someone trying to talk them into a decision that they are not prepared to make. What they really want is information.

When you buy a car, you certainly want to know what the best deals are, what the best vehicles are, how they drive and so forth. You probably do *not,* however, want some slick car salesperson coming up to talk to you about *"this little baby"* that he can get you a great deal on, right? That's exactly how most buyers feel when they're considering purchasing a home.

Think of their needs and desires first. Next, try to put those needs and desires into a strong headline that will tempt the customer into reading the rest of the article or advertisement. *"Local Couple mauled by Lion while viewing new home at Open House"* or *"Local home, haunted by Victoria Secret Model, will be open this weekend"* would probably cause a potential client to read the article, but certainly would not fit the category of filling their needs or desires.

Strong headlines that target specific potential clients might include:

Sellers:

- ❑ How to sell your home in a slow market.
- ❑ Local agent reveals guerrilla tactics for marketing homes.
- ❑ New home seller report helps local couple save thousands when selling home.
- ❑ Don't sell your home until you learn the 19 critical errors made by homeowners selling for top dollar.
- ❑ Learn 25 inexpensive repairs that could increase the value of your home with our new report.

Buyers:

- ❑ The 17 Deadly Mistakes Home Buyers make when buying their first home.
- ❑ New report reveals the secrets to buying a home with little or no money down.
- ❑ Learn the secrets of buying foreclosure homes with new report.
- ❑ Don't spend one more dime on rent until you read this new free report by industry insiders.

For Specific Groups:

- ❑ Seniors - Free report reveals methods to keep your money when moving to senior housing.
- ❑ Farm Owners - New report reveals the deadliest mistakes made by farm owners that cost them tens of thousands of dollars.
- ❑ Investors – The truth about property flipping is revealed in a new free report.
- ❑ Investors – Special tax program allows investors to sell property and pay no capital gains!

Newsworthy Marketing

Once you have the targets selected, their needs determined, and a headline crafted to target their needs, write an article that speaks to the customer emotionally. What is their pain? Why do they want to move? What are their needs and their hopes?

New Government Program Helps Allentown Buyer Purchase Home with No Money Down.

Allentown, PA - Carmen looked back at her old apartment for the last time as she loaded her car with the last of her personal belongings. Carmen had spent 3 long years in the cramped apartment with her husband and daughter, Ashley. Recently, she discovered a new government loan program...

The entire article is geared toward showing the client that they really *can* do what they want to do, if only they had a little more information, which you can provide them at absolutely no charge. Remember that buyers buy emotionally, and sellers sell emotionally. Logic, unfortunately, often plays a very small role in moving.

A buyer wants to get out of the endless loop of throwing money away in rent. The buyer wants something to call their own, to build equity, to have a yard for their children, to paint the colors they want to paint. Draw each of these into your story as you write it.

"Tears welled in Carmen's eyes as she considered the years that she spent trying to save enough money to buy a home of her own.

At one point she thought it would never happen because the bills always seemed to be greater than her income."

These articles can be used in dozens of different media. An advertisement that looks like an article can be run in the local newspaper, local homes magazine or any periodical. These stories can be turned into postcards and mailed to your target groups. An article like the example above may be mailed to renters in apartment complexes.

We've successfully used newsworthy articles in newsletters, postcards and even on the on our websites. Each story is geared to the target group, speaking emotionally to that group and their needs. Each story also offers free information to help the group accomplish the same end result as those in the story.

Free Reports

ERA Real Estate did a successful advertising campaign several years ago offering a free book or guide on how to purchase a home. Certainly, they received many calls from people who simply wanted the free book. However, they also were able to compile a list of potential clients who responded to their advertising, thereby allowing the company to begin a more targeted campaign of connecting with *those* particular clients, rather than using the shotgun approach to marketing.

Most of us can't afford to publish a book and send free copies all over creation for anyone who calls in, so we have to find a more cost effective way to achieve the same results. A simple solution is 3 to 15 page booklets or pamphlets that succinctly answer the question advertised in the article.

Unfortunately, this is where I tend to lose most agents unless I provide them with copies of these informational pamphlets. The task of actually writing 3 or 4 pages of a pamphlet seems to be too daunting for most agents. The truth, however, is that it is relatively easy to write a pamphlet and it is good practice to determine what really *is* beneficial to a potential client.

For example, you may advertise that home buyers make many mistakes that cost them thousands of dollars when buying a home. That is a true statement. Buyers hire the wrong mortgage company that gouges the client on fees. Buyers neglect to have home inspections because they want to save money and end up with significant problems. Buyers don't research the area, neighborhood or schools properly when initially purchasing, and so on.

Can you take a few minutes and write down the mistakes you've seen buyers or sellers make? Can you have lunch with a few other agents and share ideas of what mistakes buyers and sellers make?

Take the list, number the mistakes one through whatever, and write a short description of what each mistake means, why it costs home buyers money and how to avoid the mistake. Tada! You have a free report that you can advertise.

For those of you who are still outright terrified of writing reports, go to www.gooder.com. The Gooder Group has written many different free reports for Realtors and mortgage professionals and makes them available for a fee.

Some of Gooder's current informational booklets include:

- ❑ NEW HOMES: 10 Secrets You Should Know Before You Visit Your First Model Home
- ❑ PRE-INSPECT: How To Inspect A Home Before You Make An Offer
- ❑ POINTS: Sharp Ways To Make Mortgage Points Work For You
- ❑ RENT vs BUY: How To Make The Best Use Of Your Housing Dollars
- ❑ RENTALS: 7 Secrets You Must Know To Succeed As A Landlord
- ❑ SECOND HOMES: Why Now Is The Time To Buy
- ❑ SECRETS: Nine Deadly Traps To Avoid When Buying A Home
- ❑ SMART BUYING: 8 Inside Tips Every Buyer Must Know In Today's Market
- ❑ EXPIRED: How To Sell A Home That Didn't Sell
- ❑ FAST SALE: Twelve Inside Tips For A Quick Home Sale
- ❑ FIRST-TIME SELLERS: 13 Proven Secrets To Sell Your First Home Faster
- ❑ FOR SALE BY OWNER: How To Sell Your Home In Today's Market
- ❑ FORECLOSURE: How To Save Your Credit If You Can't Save Your Home
- ❑ INCENTIVES: Attract More Home Buyers With A Little Something Extra
- ❑ LUXURY PROPERTIES: 7 High-Price Mistakes Even Smart Sellers Make
- ❑ MAKEOVERS: 20 Low-Cost Ways To Drive Up Your Home's Value

Free Reports on the Internet

Web sites are really marketing, advertising and informational vehicles. Those of you who have a web site set up that simply says "Rebecca Sells Denver Homes", and has a glamour shot of you, need to re-think your online strategy.

Again, no one will call Rebecca to buy or sell a home from a simple ad saying "Rebecca sells Denver homes", and if they do, I would question their motives. When you add your properties for sale to a site, you pick up a little bit of response. You typically won't get a tremendous response because most buyers know they can go directly to Realtor.com or another large site and find everyone's listings.

A method to attract the customers viewing your website to contact you is by offering something of value. A banner on your site may offer, *"Learn 25 inexpensive repairs that could increase the value of your home with our new report."*

There are two keys to making this work. First, give enough information that the client *has to have* a copy of the report. Second, don't give it to them without getting their information. They need to fill out an online form in order to receive their copy of the report.

This information is critical because part of the process of prospecting is to identify the potential clients so you can set up a system to regularly contact those clients.

Your online form should include contact information, such as name, address, phone number and email address. The form should also allow the user to fill out a form on what they would like to purchase or sell, and ask for the time frame of their considered move.

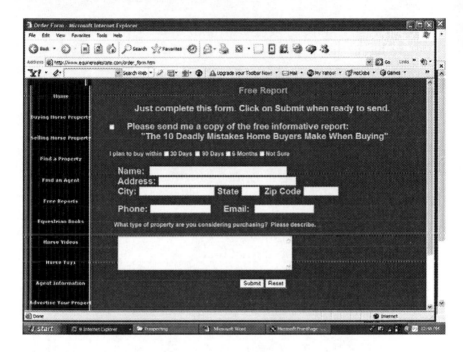

I do not believe it's necessary to ask the user to fill out some huge form with lots of information because you're more likely to cause the user to simply give up and close the window. The less information you can ask for while still learning about the prospect, the more likely you are to get them to fill out the form.

Market Evaluations

Offering free information or something of value to a client may include a no-cost or no obligation market evaluation of their property. Remember, however, that you are trying to lower the barrier of resistance. The prospect really doesn't want you coming over to their home because they believe you'll try to sell them on yourself and listing the property.

The harder you try to get in the door to meet with them, the more likely they are to believe you are a pushy salesperson. However, the person who *does* get in the door first is the most likely person to eventually get the listing, so you don't simply want to continually send information.

Giving away information helps you to build a bridge to that customer or a perceived relationship with that customer. One method of giving information without scaring the prospect is to offer a free market evaluation over the phone. This is a very risky endeavor, however, because inevitably, the customer believes their home is worth more than it truly is. If you advertise or market that you will provide free over-the-phone evaluations, you need to be careful not to actually give a specific price on the phone: *"I'm sorry, I can't be more exact without actually looking at the home, but I can certainly email you or drop off comparables in your home's size and age range for your review."*

Automatic Listing Updates

Buyers want information on properties as properties come on the market. They also don't want to be *"bothered"* by *"salespeople"* calling them. You can offer something of value by providing them with a steady flow of properties as they come on the market. Most real estate companies or multiple listings systems now have some form of an auto prospecting system which allows listings to be automatically sent to the clients based on the criteria entered in the system.

There's also a secret you should know about marketing your auto prospecting system: even though virtually every Realtor in the United States can offer this service to their clients, most home buyers don't know about it. Realtors mistakenly assume their clients know about their tools. They don't.

Because few agents are promoting their automatic listing update systems, you can market it as an exclusive tool.

New Home Seeker Computer System allows buyers to find out about homes the DAY they go on the market for sale!

A more powerful approach may be to show potential buyers that they may lose the best deals if they don't become part of some search system. Fear of loss is a far more powerful motivator than the desire for gain.

Hundreds of clients call our offices each year asking to be put on the secret list of buyers for foreclosure properties. Foreclosure listings, of course, are generally put on the open market because banks know that the open market generates a higher price than simply trying to sell to a few investors at a steep discount. Despite this fact, buyers everywhere seem to think that these "*great deals*" are being hidden.

Try to apply the same emotional technique to your automatic listing updates. What buyers want are great deals. The truth about great deals is that they seldom last on the market long enough to be advertised in homes magazines where they will be seen by many buyers. Even in slow markets, there are still "*hot*" listings.

Secret System allows some home buyers to beat everyone else to the best hot new listings!

Did you know that the very best listings never make it into Homes Magazines or the newspaper? They're scooped up by buyers with an inside track, by investors or by Realtors. Foreclosed properties, estates, and all the hottest deals in the local real estate market go fast.

Now, you may have an opportunity to become part of this exclusive club of buyers, by using a new super computer program used by Abercrombie Real Estate. The Home Seeker System allows...

You can increase your response to this program further by lowering the barrier of resistance to the prospect. As you write your article about this incredible computer system, include that the customer will not be bothered by calls from a real estate agent. The buyer can simply call you when they see a property that they may have interest in.

Even if you promise not to call, you are collecting the names and information on buyers who want to purchase. Your goal is to find a way to follow up. Be honest in your responses. When a customer emails and tells you they want to be added to the program, make a follow-up phone call to them in order to thank them for joining the system and ask questions to get a clearer picture of their needs. This accomplishes the additional task of beginning to build rapport with the client.

Agent: *"Mrs. Hall?"*

Client: *"Yes?"*

Agent: *"Hi, this is Peter Parker from the Web Agency. You filled out our online form to become part of our exclusive home seeker program. I won't take up much of your time. I wanted to thank you for filling out the form, and I just wanted to ask you a few questions to get a better picture of what you're looking for. The more information we have, the better we can program our computer to search for you. Would it be okay to ask you a few questions?"*

Using a USP – Unique Selling Proposition

A Unique Selling Proposition, as applied to a real estate agent or broker, is a position you create in the eyes of the consumer that you are unique among your peers. In other words, a consumer may come to you first because of something specific you offer.

Many real estate agents are continually frustrated by discount real estate firms. Some of these firms advertise teaser commission rates, and up-sell the customer when they figure access to the multiple listing system, advertising and buyer's agents back into the equation.

A successful full-service agent can often explain the difference between a discount broker's program and their own full-service program and list the property. However, in many cases, the full-service broker doesn't even get to play in the arena. The prospective home seller may *only* call the discount broker because their perception is that the discount broker is offering the same service at a discounted rate. This is a Unique Selling Proposition.

The same can be said of real estate agents who successfully secure a niche market, such as horse farms, historic homes or green homes. A client may call *only* the agent in the niche market because their perception is that the niche agent has more knowledge and can therefore get the property sold more quickly and for more money.

For a USP to be effective, it should be short and memorable. A USP won't work if it's a paragraph long. It should be something that can be added to your business card, your personal brochure and any other literature you send out. Your USP should be boldly listed on your website, and in marketing that you direct at the target group your USP relates to.

Unique Selling Propositions for real estate fall into four broad categories:

1 – Niche Market USP

The goal with a "Niche Market USP" is to create the image that you are *the* specialist or expert in one area of the market. For example, you could be *"The Equestrian Property Specialist"* if your niche is horse property. For seniors, you might get the Senior Relocation designation. Everything you do to that market should have a tag line that identifies you as the expert.

2 – Unique Service USP

Many agents get confused when I talk about Unique Service offers because they believe that every agent can do exactly the same things. That's true, for the most part. However, most agents don't craft marketing around the emotional hot buttons of their customers. A perfect example is the automatic listing program. *"Find out about every property the day they're listed before most buyers know they're for sale with our free home search computer system."* You are making an offer of something that is not typical of other marketing and advertising.

"Find out about foreclosed property first with Steve Furst" is a Unique Service USP. If you're the go-to person for finding loans with no money down, your USP might be *"The No Money Down Specialist"*, or *"Call to find out how to buy a home with little or no money down!"*

Another unique service approach is when you're working as part of a team. Your unique service becomes *"Hiring me is hiring a full team of expert professionals. Don't get stuck with 'just an agent'!"*

3 – Service or Performance Guarantee

Although we'll be discussing guarantees in Chapter 9, a guarantee of your service is a unique competitive advantage that will separate you from the average real estate agent. ERA has used performance guarantees very effectively in advertising. *"If your home doesn't sell, ERA will buy it!"* Customers, who may not have heard the ad for several years, still remember it.

Performance guarantees include:

- ❏ If you're unhappy with my service, you can cancel the listing at any time!
- ❏ I guarantee to sell your home in 90 days or I will charge you no listing side commission!
- ❏ If I can't sell your home in 99 days, I'll buy it!

❑　　　If I fail to call you with an update every single week, I'll give you $1000 at closing!

After reading this aggressive list of guarantees, you may be in full panic mode. Don't worry. We'll explain each and how they apply in Chapter 9.

4 – Comparison USP

"Full Service for a Reduced Commission" is a comparison USP from a discount brokerage. You can compare yourself with your competition in many ways, including:

❑　　　My listings sell for an average of 99.2% of list price!
❑　　　On average, Ted's listings sell for 2.2% MORE than other homes in the market!
❑　　　Our team's listings sell an average of 30% faster than the competition's listings!

USP Viral Marketing

One of the objects of a career in real estate is to grow your business over time. A key method of growing your business is to build a steady stream of referrals by convincing your current clients, past clients and sphere of influence to send their friends, relatives and co-workers to you.

Whether your USP's are for a particular niche market, a unique service or a performance guarantee, teaching your USP to your clients and repeating it on everything you send them will increase the likelihood that they will, in turn, repeat it to their friends and relatives. Unfortunately, we can't insure that our clients refer us regularly. We have to remind them to refer us, and we have to rely on their enthusiasm for our service and their natural desire to help their friends by referring someone that does a great job. For years, my firm has searched for ways to tap into the potential referral network of each client. Luckily, with the age of YouTube and the iPhone upon us, there are methods by which you can exponentially grow the number of prospective clients who view your unique message.

Most people now have a personal email address, and a list of email addresses of friends and relatives. If done correctly, we can now tap into this network to deliver our messages.

You probably receive several emails each week, if not several hundred, containing jokes, recipes or links to entertaining information on the web from friends, relatives and coworkers. So does everyone else. If you can convince your clients to send out information about you to their online network, and further entice the receiver to view the information, you can vastly expand your network.

What could you possibly do to entice your clients to send out your information? How can you find a way to get others to open that information? People are motivated by their own selfish desires. The selfish desire may be to sell their home, or it may be to show off the home they purchased.

Creating video is not as difficult as you might think. Adobe Premier Elements is available for less than $100 and allows you to easily import photos and video into a single movie file, which can be uploaded to YouTube or other sites for free.

New Listing Video

Start by constructing a 10 to 15 second video spot that outlines your Unique offer or service. You'll be using this on everything you email to clients.

Next, for each home you list for sale, create a short video presentation about the home. It only has to be a few minutes long. Take a nice exterior shot and some panning shots of the interior rooms. Compile them into a video.

At the very beginning of the video should be a title page that introduces the property and has your information somewhere on the screen. The next several minutes should be all about the home that your are trying to sell. The very end of the video should be where you add your 10 to 15 second offer.

Once the video is compiled, upload it to YouTube or another free hosting site on the Internet and email the link to your seller. Let the seller know that it is important to get their property in front of as many people as humanly possible, so would they please forward a copy of it to everyone in their personal email list or database.

Since there is a benefit to the home seller, they will be very likely to forward the video. Because their friends and relatives will be curious about the home and how the video looks, they will be likely to play the video. This means you are exponentially increasing the number of people who see your message.

Gorgeous Bethlehem Split for sale

For more information, call
Loren Keim
Century 21 Keim Realtors
800-648-4421

Incidentally, the fact that you are even creating a video and doing something outside the normal newspaper ads and signs to market a home conveys to the viewer that you are a hard working Realtor. When they think of selling, they'll be more likely to call you *simply because* you created the video. The additional message on the end is a bonus.

New Purchase Video

The exact same method can be applied to someone purchasing a home. Your 10 to 15 second message may be slanted toward buyers rather than sellers, but the concept is the same.

Shoot a quick video of the home your buyers are purchasing. Compile the video with an introduction slide saying something like "Welcome to Mark and Sally Smith's New Home!" along with your tag line on the bottom. The end of the video should again contain your message.

Email the link to your buyers saying that you had created the video in order for them to view the home whenever they'd like up to closing, and they may want to share it with their friends and relatives. They will likely send it on to everyone in their email list, and their friends and relatives will be curious and are likely to watch the video.

Summary

Simple marketing messages offering service, or depicting yourself as a top agent in the area are unlikely to produce many results. Every opportunity to contact potential clients is a chance to have that potential client read your message. Create a message from the perspective of what the client really wants, and give the message an emotionally powerful headline that will cause the prospect to actually read the message.

When marketing or prospecting to find potential buyers, sellers or investors, you are more likely to entice individuals to identify themselves if you offer them something of value. That something of value can be free information that is valuable to the client, such as information on avoiding mistakes in their sale or purchase, or information on special financing techniques.

Other forms of value include free evaluations of their property or free information for buyers, such as a steady flow of listings through an automatic listing program. To truly improve your results, add a unique sales message or Unique Selling Proposition that will differentiate you from your competition.

Chapter 5: Follow-Up Systems

> **Elbert Hubbard**: *"How many a man has thrown up his hands at a time when a little more patience would have achieved success."*

Everything we do in prospecting or marketing to attract potential customers is designed to get prospective clients to identify themselves. Once you create a list of people who are considering moving, you *need* to do what 95% of your competition does not: follow up.

One of the primary differences between successful mega-agents and everyone else is that mega-agents create systems into which they plug prospective clients that allow follow up with those clients.

When I started my career in real estate, I created a simple follow-up system out of index cards. I would create a 3x5 or 4x6 index card on each client and simply call through them, writing down the results on a regular basis.

The front of the card had the client information including name, address, phone number, a description of their real estate needs and other basic information. The back of the card had the dates I contacted them and the results of each conversation. If I had a client for a long period of time, I would end up stapling cards together.

The computer revolution and web based hosting has made the process much simpler. All the information you need to maintain contact with a client can be stored on your computer. Every follow-up contact can also be stored on your computer.

First, you need to start with two concepts that are often foreign to new real estate associates. The first is creating a computer database in a database or contact management program. The second is sorting that database by contact types.

Client Databases

If you don't have your clients organized in some form of electronic database, you need to go get one as quickly as possible. This database may be an online program, such as Top Producer, or it may be a program you purchase and install in your computer, such as ACT.

Unless you have some sort of contact management software, you'll be trying to maintain contact with your clients by hand and will be less able to compete with those agents who are more computer savvy. Any contact management program will have a list of your clients, along with their contact information.

Your clients should be grouped into different categories. Some successful agents use simple groupings of "A", "B" and "C" buyers and sellers based on their motivation and ability.

I have a rather large database, so I attempt to differentiate them in several ways. My primary distinction in groups is by a combination including the type of property and client. For example, some of the categories I use are: *"Horse Farm – Buyer"*, *"Horse Farm – Seller"*, *"Investor"*, *"Current Listing"*, *"Sphere of Influence."*, and *"Past Client – Buyer"*.

Some contacts have several different contact types. Someone in my sphere of influence may also be an investor or a current listing. These categories allow me to send targeted mailings or e-mailings just to the group that will value the mailings.

For example, I send out several e-newsletters. One is targeted specifically at real estate investors. All my marketing to this group has a specific theme and includes free reports and a USP that targets that group. My sphere of influence, on the other hand, receives fun mailings that still include free reports, but a very different USP. Farm buyers and sellers make up a third group that receive newsletters targeted at what's happening in the farm communities and how they're being impacted, and offers reports that service that direct group.

Customers in multiple categories may receive a variety of mailing or e-mailing pieces from me.

Adding to your database

Your income in real estate will be in proportion to the number of people you connect with regularly. Each time you come in contact with someone is an opportunity to build your sphere of influence and your database. As you meet people, whether in a real estate setting or in a social setting, you can ask them if you may keep in touch.

Agent: *"Hey, it was great meeting you today. By the way, from time to time, I send my friends and clients information on the real estate market. Would you be interested in receiving it?"*

This method can be used with your hair stylist, your auto mechanic, your doctor or anyone you see on a regular basis. This is a non-threatening approach to getting their permission to stay in touch. My experience is that most people will agree, and you'll be able to continually build your network.

Drip Systems

Far too many of my trainees over the years have mailed to a large group once or twice only to complain that mailing doesn't work, because no one responded. It's true that mailing is not nearly as effective as phone calling or door knocking for your initial foray into the world of prospecting. However, mailing is a very good follow-up to keep in touch, as long as it's done consistently over time, and directed at people you've physically spoken with.

Have you ever visited a cave or cavern and had the tour guide explain that stalactites and stalagmites are really just mineral deposits from water slowly dripping on one spot over time? Any good contact management program that you purchase and use effectively will accomplish the same task. Over time, you're planting seeds about yourself and your business.

Each contact, whether by mail, phone, e-mail or in person, will help to build your long-term relationship with that person you're contacting. The most important facet of the process is laying out a system and continuing to follow it.

I've found that in my own business, when I get very busy, I forget to send out mailers, newsletters and I stop maintaining contact with my database. My business slowly goes down like a balloon with a slow air leak. When I begin reconnecting with the database, leads re-appear and my business increases.

To avoid this up-and-down cycle, you should plan out any system a minimum of 90 days in advance. If you plan on using a mix of newsletters, e-mails and personal hand written notes, then plan your activities for specific dates over the next 90 days. Write all the newsletters at the same time, if possible, so you simply have to send them or put them in the mail with very little thought.

Newsletters

There are positives and negatives to any follow-up system. One of the most popular methods agents use to keep in touch with their database is the use of newsletters. The positive to sending newsletters to clients is that they *are* receiving regular information from you. The negative is that most agents are sending very generic newsletters that hit the garbage can before they are opened.

There are many ready-prepared real estate newsletters that can be purchased with your name and contact information printed on them for a nominal charge. The best of these prepared newsletters have a variety of information, articles, reasons to call you for free information, response cards and even contests to keep the reader involved.

Services that offer customized, ready-prepared real estate newsletters include:

- ❑ The Gooder Group (www.gooder.com)
- ❑ Real Estate Marketing Products (www.reamark.com)
- ❑ Ready to Go (www.readytogonewsletters.com)
- ❑ TMA Farmnet (www.tmafarmnet.com)
- ❑ Many others

If you're going to use newsletters as part of your ongoing contact program, you might consider taking the time to personally write articles that are meaningful to your clients. Information on local zoning, local legal issues, and the local market are far more likely to be read by your database.

Writing your own newsletter also allows you the opportunity to insert articles that advertise more free reports or other free information. This again allows prospective clients to contact you as *the* source for real estate info.

E-Newsletters

As with physical newsletters, there are positives and negatives to e-newsletters. Email and e-news are actually even less likely to be read than the physical version. This is because the public has become spam-weary. There is so much junk coming through our email that we actively delete email, without opening them.

The bright side to e-newsletters is that they are very inexpensive to send, and far easier to get to your prospects than labeling and stamping physical newsletters.

Just like physical newsletters, there are many good sources where you can buy ready-prepared real estate specific newsletters. Some real estate franchises actually provide e-newsletters for their agents. Century 21, for example, offers several free customizable newsletters monthly that can be sent out to your database. They include a general one for buyers and sellers called *"Life at Home"* and specific ones targeted at commercial real estate, investors and luxury properties.

Testimonial Letters

One of the most effective communications a potential client can receive is a third-party endorsement of your service. In other words, if you have a very satisfied client who is willing to write their experiences in a letter to you, you can copy the letter or parts of the letter into a brochure, a mailing or an e-mailing.

If the message is emotionally charged and specifically outlines what you were able to accomplish for the client, your response will be even better.

For example, we had a client a number of years ago who was ordered by the court to have a permanent home that he owned within twenty days or he would lose custody of his daughter. Even with slightly shaky credit, we were able to put together a sale with no money down and get him to settlement in time. He wrote us a very powerful letter, which helped us to grow our business.

In the beginning of your career, you may not have any great stories of your accomplishments. See if you can "borrow" stories from other agents, and simply use the agency name with your name at the bottom. *"And that's how I saved my home with the help of Elvis Pancake Realtors. If you need assistance with your home sale, please call Agatha Berman at ..."*

Another way to obtain testimonials is to contact all the mortgage lenders and title companies that frequent your real estate office. Ask if they'll write you a third-party endorsement letter. Since they want your business, they're usually very happy to write about what a wonderful real estate professional you are!

Evidence of Success Pieces

I ran into one of my clients in a grocery store last year. He had bought his personal residence from me and bought and sold investment property with me. He mentioned that he was planning to sell a dry cleaning service that he owned. I, of course, asked if he'd like me to look at it. He replied that he had already listed with a competing firm. *"You don't do any commercial real estate, though, do you? I would have used you."*

By that point, I had not only sold other laundry businesses, but had sold several dozen commercial properties and even written a successful book about selling commercial real estate. That doesn't mean that my clients knew what I had done.

Don't expect everyone in your database to know everything that you do. You have to show them what you do. One method of showing them is to write short stories about clients you assisted in various aspects of real estate. Explain how you assisted someone with poor credit to improve their credit and own a home, or assisted someone in getting top dollar for their small bakery.

A series of different postcards or short letters should be designed to show the breadth of your experience in selling real estate and examine ways you may be able to assist your clients. Some suggestions of evidence of success pieces might show how you:

❑ Helped a first-time buyer.
❑ Assisted a buyer in finding low money down mortgage programs.
❑ Helped to market or sell a commercial property.
❑ Sold a luxury home.
❑ Helped an empty nester move down to a smaller home.
❑ Any other story you can think up.

As you write these stories, they will resonate differently with your client database. Your sister may be thinking of you every time someone talks about selling a home, but she may not have thought of you when her best friend from college talked about investing in a property or buying with no money down. A story may ring a bell in the back of her mind and cause her to contact you and her friend and create a referral.

Ten years ago, I joined a networking organization known as Le-Tip. Le-Tip is a networking organization that allows only one person from any particular industry to join, such as one realtor, one mortgage officer, one electrician, one day care owner, one dentist and one professional clown.

At the end of each meeting, we each stand up and give 30 second commercials about what we do. For years, I simply said "*I sell real estate.*" I had the mistaken belief that everyone would understand what that meant. More recently, I've found that if I tell very short stories about different kinds of transactions, they are more likely to refer more business. Stories resonate with listeners, and better explain the breadth of your experience.

Again, you should plan any attack strategy at least 90 days in advance, so it makes sense to pick out several stories that showcase various aspects of your business and write the postcards all at once. Then simply lay out a time frame to send them.

Mixing and Matching

Once you've identified prospective future clients, you'll need to begin building a relationship with them. In general, relationships are based on individuals liking and trusting one another. It is difficult to make someone like and trust you simply by mailing "stuff" to them. However, you can build a relationship that provides value to the prospective client. Continue to give the prospect good information in small increments, and the opportunity to respond to the information or request more.

Many of the most successful real estate professionals use a variety of techniques to maintain communication with their sphere of influence, past clients and target markets and to deliver value to those potential clients. Newsletters may be effective with certain people, and may be simply thrown out, unread, by others.

Evidence of success postcards, testimonial letters, e-mails and e-newsletters may be interspersed with newsletters in order to capture the highest readership level.

Integrating Your Online and Offline Prospecting Strategies

Several database management programs allow Realtors to easily integrate their online and offline strategies. The key to success is communication through a mix of contact methods. Using a combination of postcards, emails containing links, letters, and personal contact is far more effective communication with your database than simply using a single method of maintaining contact.

Programs such as Top Producer allow the user to set up "Action Plans" or "Action Sequences" that assist an agent in keeping in touch with their sphere of influence or other target audiences.

An "Action Plan" is a series of events or reminders that help to keep you, the agent, on track in your communications. While these plans have relevance in every area of your real estate career, they have particular importance to prospecting.

Action plans are predetermined timelines that can contain pre-written letters, emails, postcards and reminders to make phone calls. These action plans can be set up to utilize each of these forms of contact at certain intervals.

In many real estate contact management programs, an agent may select an action plan to apply to a particular client that may automatically send out emails at certain intervals, prompt the agent to print prewritten letters and envelopes, and remind the agent to make calls.

An example for a home owner who may consider selling in 60 days might contain the following:

1. The Day the plan is applied, automatically email a note thanking the home owner for discussing their plans with you, the agent.
2. Five Days after plan is applied, automatically email a note explaining the agent's guarantee program.
3. Ten Days after plan is applied, prompt the agent to send "Seller Prospecting Letter 1" in the mail.
4. Fifteen Days after plan is applied, prompt agent to make a follow-up call to the seller.
5. Twenty Days after plan is applied, automatically email a note explaining the agent's marketing and advertising program.
6. Twenty Five Days after plan is applied, prompt agent to send "Seller Prospecting Letter 2" in the mail.
7. Thirty Days after plan is applied, prompt agent to call the seller again to follow up on their plans.
8. Thirty Five Days after plan is applied, automatically email a note with an Evidence of Success story.
9. Forty Days after the plan is applied, prompt the agent to send Seller Postcard 1.
10. Forty Five Days after the plan is applied, prompt the agent to make another phone call to the seller.

In the case of Top Producer, the emails may be prewritten and set up to be automatically sent. Each user has a dashboard with a list of the day's activities. If the activities include ten letters that need to be sent out, a simple click of the mouse allows the letters to be sent to the printer, followed by envelopes if you desire.

Below is a screen shot of some of Top Producer's *"campaigns"*, which are great action sequences that can provide a mix of contact methods with potential clients.

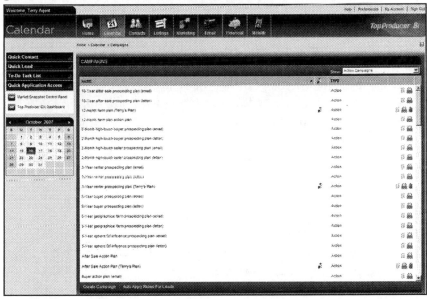

Screen Shot of Top Producer software showing some available Action Plans.

Humor

Additionally, humor can be part of any follow-up campaign. Although many Realtors and real estate trainers "pooh-pooh" it as being unprofessional, humor can obviously work in attracting attention. Your goal is to always set yourself apart from the competition. Running the same homes magazine ads week after week will get you exactly the same results as everyone else's homes magazine ads.

Humor can be an ice breaker with your potential clients. For those of you who are skeptics and nay-sayers, let me pose a question. Which car insurance company comes to mind first when you want to save money on car insurance?

As I wrote earlier, I've run ads like *"Loren Keim – Outstanding in his field"* with a photo of me in the middle of a farmer's field. Agents across the country run similar ads. Humorous messages you may have seen in your own marketplace include *"List your home with me, and I'll get right on it"* with a photo of the agent sitting on top of the house. I've seen several variations of ads that feature a Realtor sitting or kneeling next to their favorite dog. The captions all read something like: *"Trustworthy, Dependable and Loyal... and so is the dog."*

These ads and many like them have been run by Realtors across the country. Those Realtors who have the most success with comedic advertising tell us that the key is to make fun of yourself in a positive way. Self deprecating humor, when done correctly, can evoke a strong positive emotional response.

However, when using humor, carefully analyze your audience. Messages that are too corny may generate a negative reaction depending on your target audience for the message. Additionally, make sure your message is not just humorous, but clearly indicates what you do and why you're exceptional. Too many agents believe that the humor alone will make a customer call. This can't be further from the truth. Every ad must have a clear and strong message associated with it.

In Geico commercials, the humorous tag line is *"I just saved a lot of money by switching to Geico."* The ad is funny and entertaining, yet the message is very strong, precise and clear.

Promotional Items

Many agents use promotional items in order to stand out in the crowd, and also to provide the prospect with something memorable. The agent's goal is to have the prospect think of the agent when they make the buying or selling decision.

Promotional items do not have to be expensive to be effective. Our most effective mailer includes a magnetic calendar with a tear-off page for each of the 12 months. These calendars retail for around 30 cents a piece, and stay on your prospect's and client's refrigerators for a whole year.

The shear number of times a client has mentioned *"I see you every day on my refrigerator"* has convinced me that this is the single best item I send out each year.

Agents in my firm send out everything from personalized pens, refrigerator magnets, key chains and jar openers to larger items like baseball caps, day planners and coffee mugs. Each item should be carefully considered to meet your budget and to deliver the proper message.

For example, a key chain may be thrown in a drawer and forgotten. A jar opener may also be placed in a drawer, but may be pulled out each time they need to open that pickle jar! Day planners, while expensive on a per planner basis, may be something the client will use every day for the entire year, and they could be looking at your name and message on the front.

Our agents have had fun with some of the items they've ordered. For example, Bonnie and Marlene, from our Allentown Marketing Center, ordered Fortune Cookies with personalized messages. They very carefully wrote uplifting fortune cookie messages that dealt with the home, and then put their contact information on the reverse side of the message. When purchased in bulk, a box containing 4 personalized fortune cookies cost less than 60 cents.

These boxes, pictured below, were a very inexpensive marketing project that was used as a follow up to "*For Sale by Owners*", although they could have been used in Geographic Farming or with your Sphere of Influence.

4 Fortune Cookies with personalized messages and a box cost one of our agents less than a dollar a piece.

Popular Specialty items, imprinted with your name or your company name include:

- Seed packets for the Spring
- Personalized Pens / Pencils
- Rulers
- Measuring Tapes
- Baseball Hats
- Balloons
- Day Planners
- Desk Calendars
- Magnetic Cards
- Key tags

- 97 -

- Bottle Openers
- Wine Corks
- House shaped stress squeezies
- Emery boards
- House shaped letter openers
- Welcome mats
- And Many others

There are many online and catalog providers of specialty products. The one I've had the most luck with is **Don Blose** and **Gideon Specialties**. His firm takes the time to assist you in selecting the right product, and developing a message that resonates with your clients. Gideon's website is www.GideonPromotionalProducts.com and their phone number for a personal, no-cost consultation is 610-392-9149.

Chapter 6: Initial Long Term Prospecting Methods

James Austin: "Chance favors those in motion."

Long term prospecting involves the creation of a client base or a database of clients, consistently staying in touch with that client base, and offering them your services. The good news is that when long term prospecting is done correctly, it generally provides consistent business to you year after year. The bad news is that typical long term prospecting methods take 12-18 months to produce their first result.

Many Realtors begin their careers by trying to use *only* long term prospecting methods to be successful. They do long term prospecting so that they don't have to actually pick up the phone and call anybody. One of the many problems with this scenario is that the new agent attempts to run a long term campaign for 4-8 months and then gives up before it actually begins to work.

There are many forms of long term prospecting. Some methods include Geographic farming, demographic farming, and sphere of influence farming. As I mentioned in the first chapter, I suggest starting your career by selecting two different target groups. One should be your sphere of influence because they already like and trust you.

Sphere of Influence

You probably know at least 100 people that you see from time to time. You have family, friends, old acquaintances, former co-workers, college roommates and even the doctor, dentist and hair dresser that you see on a regular basis. You may not realize it, but these people are the beginning of your client base. As your career grows, you'll add past clients, business associates and new contacts to this client base.

Agents often don't realize that their 68 year old Uncle Charlie could possibly assist them in the listing or sale of a luxury home or a multi-million dollar office building. The truth is that every person you know has their own internal database of people they connect with regularly. This group of people is *their* sphere of influence. Your goal is to hopefully convince your sphere to use you in every real estate transaction, and also to leverage your relationships by tapping into *their* sphere of influence.

Almost 20 years ago, I met a man named Larry, who was living in a roach-infested tenement in Easton, Pennsylvania. This man referred me to clients who owned several hundred properties in Pennsylvania. You will never know who you can connect with until you start asking for help from those around you.

Also, you already know people who own homes, rental units or operate small businesses. You'll never know precisely when your cousin Otto is going to sell his home or even his Scandinavian Restaurant. And wouldn't you be crushed if Otto listed his property with the Realtor across the street from your office, who has diarrhea of the mouth, because he didn't remember you were in real estate? Don't let that happen - stay in front of your sphere of influence!

And please avoid saying, *"I don't need to send anything to my family and friends. They all <u>know</u> what I do."* Because they really have no idea what you do. The truth is that as much as your Aunt Petunia likes you, at this point in your career, she's probably not going to refer you to her old high school boyfriend who is now President of the local bank.

Why? Unfortunately, Aunt Petunia, like all your relatives and friends, remembers you from your prior career. She can't visualize you as a successful real estate professional and she doesn't want to hurt her present relationships by telling them about an unproven new realtor.

It's not that Aunt Petunia and Uncle Charlie don't love you. They do. But they are afraid that if you, as a new realtor, make a mistake, it will come back to haunt them. One of our most successful techniques at my firm has been to assist agents in appearing successful before they actually <u>are</u> successful. This technique involves

Sphere of Influence Prospecting

Step 1 – Compile a list of 100 acquaintances.

Step 2- Get their addresses, phone numbers and email (if possible) and enter them into a database.

Step 3 – Write an initial letter explaining you're in Real Estate and need their help finding clients.

Step 4 – Follow up in 2 weeks with a "Properties for Sale" flyer.

Step 5 – Follow up in 2 more weeks with a "Recent Sales" flyer.

Step 6 – Send everyone a personal handwritten note in the first 90 days.

Step 7 – Schedule ongoing mailings.

keeping you in front of your sphere of influence, but also showing your sphere of influence some evidence of production.

As we outlined in the last chapter, you'll need to create a database of all those people you have some contact with. Collect all the names, addresses, phone numbers and email addresses for everyone that knows you. Enter that information into a database program or contact management program. The key, again, is to get a database put together quickly so that you can begin contacting the database consistently.

First, you need to announce that you have entered the exciting world of real estate, and second, you'll need to convince your sphere that you are the "go-to" person for anyone needing assistance. We recommend that during your first 90 days in the business, you contact your sphere 6 times, or about once every two weeks. After your initial 90 days, you should follow up with your sphere at least once a month, if not more.

Your initial letter should be simple and to the point (like the one on the next page).

Your second letter should show some evidence that you are actually working to sell properties. Honestly, by your second or third week in the industry, it's unlikely you'll have any listings, so you'll need to "borrow" some. You're going to send out a flyer that displays two or three different properties for sale, with your name and company name on the bottom of the flyer. You don't actually say anywhere that they are your listings, but your sphere of influence will assume they are, and their impression of you will hopefully shift. The reaction you're looking for is *"Wow, John seems to be doing well after only a few weeks"*.

Dear Aunt Petunia,

As you may know, I've made a career change. I'm now a licensed Real Estate Agent and I've affiliated with one of the top firms in Eastern Pennsylvania, Century 21 Keim Realtors.

In order to obtain my license, I had to take several courses over the past few months and a State Exam. To join Century 21 Keim, I've had to complete a lot of additional education, but I think it's all been worth it. Real Estate is an exciting business!

I'm hoping you'll help support me in my new endeavor. If you hear of anyone thinking of buying or selling property, please call me. I'll include a few of my business cards with this letter. Please put them in your wallet or purse and give them out to anyone you can.

Remember, although I may be new to the industry, I've had a lot of education and training, and I'm backed by some of the top people in Real Estate here at Century 21 Keim.

Thanks!

Ask around your office to find out if anyone would mind if you send copies of other agent's listings with your name on them to your clients. It's rare that an agent will tell you that they don't want you exposing their property to a few hundred people in your database.

Do you know a buyer for any of these homes?

New Parkland Colonial! The Chesterfield in Rising Sun Farms. This fabulous home features 4 ample sized bedrooms, 4 full baths , 1st floor study with area for center family room with gas fireplace, custom Kitchen w/ Cherry cabinets & granite counter tops, Master retreat with sumptuous master bath . Upgrades incl: stone and stucco front, 3 car side entry garage, 42 inch kitchen cabinets, GE appliances, and more! **$519,900**

Sansom Valley Estates - Live in luxury! This newly painted 2 story colonial has hrdwd flrs throughout! 4 BRs, 2.5 Baths, mod eat-in kitchen, dining rm, living room, family room, finished full basement! Pellet stove in liv rm and fireplace in fam rm are sure to keep you warm and cozy! Family room walks out to back yard patio. Back yard is fenced in for privacy, and contains above ground pool, with newly refinished deck. **$294,900.**

Country Bi-Level - Beautiful Bi-Level with lots of room to roam. This 3 bedroom, 1.5 bath bi-level has everything you need. A new Florida room, a 2 car garage and a above ground pool all on a 1 acre lot. Priced at just **$179,900**

For More Information, Please call:
Loren & Theresa Keim
Century 21 Keim Realtors
800-648-4421

At this point, you should begin sending personal notes to everyone you know. Purchase a few boxes of blank note cards from your local office supply store. Then set up a time each morning to write 5-10 personal handwritten notes. If you send out 5 each day, you'll hit 100 people in your database in just 20 work days. Your goal is to let them know you're thinking of them, and personally ask them for assistance.

One of the other surprising things I've discovered of top agents across the country is that almost all the top agents I've met follow a regiment of sitting down every morning between 7:30 and 9:00 and writing out between 5 and 20 personal handwritten notes. Personal notes really connect and resonate with people. If you plan to continue the practice after your initial wave of notes to your sphere of influence, you may have to really think hard each day of who you want to write to, but it will keep you in the forefront of many people's minds.

Sample personal notes:

> Hi!
>   I was just going through my files today, and realized how long it's been since I spoke with you! I love working with fun people like you...

> Hi!
>   Thanks for considering using my services, it really means a lot to me...

> Hi!
>
> I was thinking about you today, so I thought I'd write you a quick note. I just wanted to say thanks for all the little things you do for others…

> Hi!
>
> I'm waiting for a client at the office today and have a few extra minutes. I thought I'd jot you a quick note.
>
> Thanks so much for speaking with me the other day. It's truly refreshing to work with considerate people.

About two weeks after sending the initial flyer with 3 properties for sale, try sending a similar one that displays 3 sold properties. The headline of this flyer could read "*Successful Sales by Our Team!*" and the tag line on the bottom of the flyer could say "*If you know of anyone thinking of selling a home, land or investment property, please have them contact me.*" Again, even though you are honestly telling people that your firm sold the homes on the flyer; your sphere of influence will naturally read this to say that you just sold 3 homes.

This will lead to your family and friends talking about how well you're doing in such a short period of time. Again, your entire goal is to convince them that you are the person to refer, and this will typically do it. Build on your initial letters with similar marketing pieces over the first year. Keep in constant contact with this group, and add to the group continually as you meet new people.

Creating Your Sphere of Influence List

Anyone you know can be part of your sphere of influence list. That includes your family and friends, old acquaintances from work, school or life in general. Anyone you see on a regular basis, whether it's your doctor, hair dresser or the guy at the local pizza joint, should also be included on your list.

One way to grow the list over time is to ask permission to mail a few things to them. Tell them you'll be sending valuable information. This will help them to visualize you as a professional real estate agent rather than a client of theirs.

You: *"Hey, Becky, you are the best hair dresser in the entire Silicon Valley area. My hair looks great."*

Becky: *"Thanks."*

You: *"No, thank **you**. By the way, I realize you see a lot of customers every week. You **do** know I'm in Real Estate, right?"*

Becky: *"Sure, I think you mentioned it."*

You: *"Well, we have a great program right now where we're sending out information on the market and sometimes some items of value to our best friends and customers. Would you mind if I added you to the list?"*

Becky: *"No, that's great."*

You: *"Should I use your address here at the salon, or send it to your home?"*

Over the next few pages are some memory teasers of people in different job professions. Glance through the list and try to think of anyone you might know or any past acquaintances that have these occupations. Then write them down, find their current mailing address and add them to your database!

Accountant	Interior Decorator
Actor / Actress	Janitor
Administrator	Jeweler
Aerobics Instructor	Jockey
Air Traffic Controller	Judge
Ambassador	Junk Dealer
Amusement Park Worker	Karaoke Buddy
Anthropologist	Karate Trainer
Apartment Manager	Kitchen Cabinet Maker
Appraiser	Kitchen Installer
Archer	Lab Technician
Architect	Landscaper
Arms Merchant	Lawyer
Art Dealer	Librarian
Artist	Locksmith
Assembly Worker	Lumberjack
Assistant	Machinist
Astronomer	Magician
Astronaut	Maid
Auctioneer	Manicurist
Author	Marriage Counselor
Auto Mechanic	Mary Kay Rep
Auto Worker	Masseuse
Avon Lady	Mechanical Engineer
Backhoe Operator	Mercenary
Baggage Handler	Military Officer
Baker	Mobile Home Dealer
Banker	Mold Tester
Barber	Mom

Bartender
Beer Distributor
Bird Watcher
Book Dealer
Bookkeeper
Bowling Buddy
Brain Surgeon
Bus Driver
Business Executive
Business Owner
Butcher
Butler
Cab Driver
Car Pool Buddy
Carpenter
Carpet Cleaner
Caterer
Chauffeur
Chef
Chemical Engineer
Chimney Sweep
Chiropractor
Civil Engineer
Civil Servant
Class Instructor
Cleaning Person
Clown (Class)
Clown (Professional)
College Professor
Columnist
Computer Programmer
Concierge
Concrete Contractor
Congressional Aide
Congressman
Congresswoman
Construction Worker
Cosmetologist

Mortgage Officer
Mother-in-law
Mover (Beer Drinking Friend)
Mover (Professional)
Musician
New Car Salesperson
Nightclub Performer
Nightclub Owner
Novelist
Nudist
Nurse
Nurses Aid
Oil Delivery Guy
Ophthalmologist
Painter
Paramedic
Party Planner
Paving Contractor
Pediatrician
Pharmacist
Photojournalist
Physician
Physicist
Pianist
Pilot
Pizza Delivery Guy
Plastic Surgeon
Plumber
Podiatrist
Police Officer
Politician (Corrupt)
Politician (Honest)
Postal Worker
Priest
Printer
Prison Guard
Proctologist
Professional Athlete

Criminal
Dental Hygienist
Dentist
Dermatologist
Detective
Developer
Dietician
Drill Sergeant
Economist
Electrical Engineer
Electrician
Entertainers (Adult)
Entertainers (Kids)
Executive
Executive Secretary
Exterminator
Factory Worker
Farm Hand
Farmer
Fashion Designer
Firefighter
Fisherman
Fitness Trainer
Flight Attendant
Florist
Football Player
Forest Ranger
Funeral Director
Gardener
General Contractor
Golf Caddie
Golf Pro
Grocer
Gynecologist
Hair Dresser
Handyman
Health Care Worker
Heart Surgeon

Psychiatrist
Psychologist
Psychotherapist
Publisher
Radio Personality
Rancher
Receptionist
Referee
Rental Agent
Reporter
Restaurant Owner
Restaurant Server
Rock Star
Roofer
Scientist
Security Guard
Septic Inspector
Sex Therapist
Shoe Repairman
Social Worker
Song Writer
Sports Announcer
Steel Worker
Stenographer
Stock Broker
Stone Mason
Super Hero
Surveyor
Tailor
Teachers (your kid's)
Teachers (yours)
Telemarketer
Termite Inspector
Therapist
Train Conductor
Travel Agent
Tree Surgeon
Truck Driver

Home Inspector
Hotel Owner
House Wife
Insurance Salesperson

Used Car Salesman
Veterinarian
Wall Paper Hanger
Wedding Planner

Client Gatherings

In this industry, like many others, you need to create a steady flow of referrals in order to keep your business going. You need to survive long enough to create that flow of referrals. Real Estate is a relationship game. The stronger your relationships, the more referrals you will generate and the stronger bonds you'll make. Don't fall into the trap of selling a property and neglecting the client after the sale. Your clients can be your strongest advocates in this industry.

Your ongoing mail program will go a long way toward building those relationships, but there's nothing quite like the personal touch of getting together with your clients periodically. As I've talked to super producers around the country over the years, one of the common elements I've found is that super producers typically have regular client events. Some have yearly summer picnics for their clients. Others have holiday parties, or even a movie night periodically where they buy 200 tickets at a discount. The important part of the equation is regularly finding a way to be physically in front of your clients. If you don't yet have dozens of past clients, have a sphere of influence gathering, but consider giving something away that displays your profession.

One of our top agents started doing a summer picnic at her home for her friends and clients the first year she was in business. She has expressed that it's one of the greatest

things she does for her business. Not only does she have fun
and enjoy the company of her clients away from business,
but her phone rings with referrals after every client
gathering. She has now started doing a winter wine and
cheese get together as well so that she touches the group
twice a year.

Chapter 7: Short Term Prospecting Methods

Kevin W. McCarthy: *"Fear of failure or success is one and the same. Both are fear of exposure. Not of our strengths, but of our weaknesses."*

Dennis Waitley: *"There never was a winner, who wasn't a beginner."*

All of the methods in Long Term Prospecting are effective at building lasting relationships with clients that can help your career to blossom, as long as you continue to deliver good service to your customers. However, in order to stay in the business long enough for the long term methods to work for you, you'll need to generate an income by creating some short term business. You need to make it a priority to find buyers and sellers who want to buy or sell right now. If you don't, in six or seven months your spouse will be telling you that you'd better go out and get, yes, you guessed it, "a real job".

Short term systems include prospecting expired listings, properties that are "for sale by the owners", and just plain cold calling or door knocking to find the people that need to move now.

Cold Calling

I realize the absolute most avoided activity in the real estate industry is cold calling. However, if you don't have a large book of business currently, including lots of listings and a regular stream of buyers or investors knocking down your door, you need to start building a career somewhere.

Cold calling is one of the most effective methods of prospecting for several reasons. First, it is a direct method of contact. You are physically speaking with someone who may become a client. Secondly, it is incredibly inexpensive compared to other methods. Mailing letters requires paying the cost of printing, the cost of mailing and possibly even the cost of the purchase of a mailing list. Mailing specialty items or promotional items can cost even more.

Third, cold calling is the fastest way to locate clients. It takes time to prepare a mailer, prepare the mailing list, get the piece to the post office and wait for the delivery before you have any hope of a response. Picking up the phone and calling people takes almost no time, and can generate immediate clients.

Start by selecting a few target markets and then think up a reason to call them, preferably offering something of value to them. For example, your firm may have recently sold a home in a quiet suburban neighborhood nearby. Ask the listing associate if he or she minds if you prospect that particular neighborhood for other homes to sell. Chances are that the agent probably won't do it himself. Next, make a list of all the homes within a certain radius of the sold property, and locate the owners' phone numbers.

No, I didn't say locate the owners' mailing address. Again, remember that most mail will be thrown out without being opened. In order to survive in this industry, you need to find business now. Pick up the phone and start calling the home owners in the surrounding neighborhood. Keep in mind that you may be helping the property owner by giving them an update on what homes are selling for in the area.

"But, Loren – we're not allowed to call anyone anymore. Haven't you heard of the Do Not Call List?"

Cross reference the list and don't call those you're not permitted to call. Again, there are plenty of people who are not part of the do not call list. If too many people in the neighborhood are part of the 'Do Not Call' list, then you may have to resort to door knocking.

Elements of a Cold Call

There are four key elements to a cold call for real estate, and a fifth element if the call recipient asks for information:

1. Identify the person you're calling.
2. Identify yourself and your company.
3. Give the reason or objective of your call.
4. Ask a question or a qualifying statement.
5. Close for an appointment.

Any cold call should begin with identifying the person you're calling. This accomplishes two tasks. First, it catches the person's attention, and second, it identifies that you are speaking with your intended potential customer. If, for example, you were calling a neighborhood out of a cross-indexing program in order to talk to neighbors about a home you sold on the street, you will find your script will not work if the phone number now belongs to someone who does not live in the neighborhood.

The second part of any cold calling script should identify you and your company. I realize there are telemarketing workshops that explain reasons for holding back information on yourself in order to prolong a call. I believe any relationship needs to begin with honesty. Identify yourself.

The third element is the reason for your call. A reason to call might be to let the person that you're calling know that their neighbor's home has sold, or it may be as simple as a public service announcement like *"remember to change your batteries in your smoke detector."*

The final required element is to ask a question or make a qualifying statement. *"Do you know of anyone in the neighborhood who might be considering selling?"* If you're making a public service announcement, you may want to complete the call with a simple tag about your company *"And remember Over the Top Realty for all your real estate needs"*. This is a very ineffective close because it does not give the potential prospect the option to respond to you, and does not give the potential prospect any reason to prolong the conversation.

Once you've asked a question, stop talking until the receiver answers. If they come back with an affirmative response such as *"I was thinking of selling my home. What did the Johnson's get for their home?"* you now have a prospect. Try to set an appointment to meet with the person you called to give them an idea of the value of their home in the current market.

A simple direct script always works best:

> *"Hi, Mrs. Jones? This is Simon Bonaparte calling from At Your Service Realty. I'm just calling because we recently sold your neighbor's home on Prospect Avenue. The home was a beautiful split level style, and we have had calls from other buyers interested in the area. I'm just calling to see if you know of anyone else in the neighborhood that might be considering selling their home as well."*

If the home owner you're speaking with asks you how much the home sold for, there is a good chance they may be considering selling their own home within the next year or so. Make sure to follow up with a Personal Note Card and thank them for being so pleasant on the phone.

Another approach that is also simple and direct is:

> *"Hi, Mr. Smith? This is William Shakespeare calling from Your Friendly Neighborhood Real Estate Firm. I'm trying to find homes for my firm to market. I was just wondering if you were considering selling yours."*

Cold Calling for Buyers

Prospecting for potential buyers can be done in a similar straightforward approach, or with the announcement of a special program. Potential buyers can be found in rental properties. One method of attacking this market is to use a criss-cross directory or a cross reference database of apartment complexes.

An approach might be:

> *"Hi, Mr. DeCarlo? This is Mohammed Ali calling from Big Dudes Real Estate. I'm calling because I'm looking for renters who are considering taking advantage of the current real estate market and becoming home owners. We have some great deals right now. Are you planning to buy a home this year?"*

Another approach is to call with exciting news.

> *"Hi, Mr. Arbergast? This is Clark Kent calling from the Daily Realtor. I'm calling to let you know about an exciting new mortgage program that can get you into a home of your own with only $1600 total cash out of pocket and a payment of less than you're currently paying for rent. If you could own your own home instead of giving your landlord money every month and do it for less than you're paying right now, would you consider buying?"*

In order for the latter script to work, you'll need to meet with a few mortgage brokers or bankers and find the best low down payment programs. You'll also need to find out what the average tenant is paying in the complex you're about to call, and what type of home they can own for a similar or lower payment.

Creative Cold Calling

One of the top agents in our firm started cold calling right out of the starting gate. His first day in our Allentown office, he sat down and told me that he had four kids to feed.

He selected all the multi-family properties in one particular
zip code and simply called them.

> *"Hi, Mr. Oswald? My name is Rob Evans. I'm a
> real estate investor in the area. I'm actually also an
> investment specialist at Century 21 Keim Realtors.
> I'm sorry to bother you, but I noticed you owned
> some property near mine. I was wondering if you
> were considering adding to your portfolio by buying
> more properties, or if you were considering
> liquidating – selling off properties while the market is
> fairly hot?"*

This was a strong approach because many investors are
either planning to add more properties to their portfolios or
start selling off what they own. Using this script, Rob was
able to find both property buyers and property sellers with
one set of phone calls. The cold calling technique helped
him to jump-start his career.

Voice Mail and Answering Machines

In today's society, many people screen their calls. I once
heard real estate super trainer Brian Buffini refer to the
answering machine as the moat that protects a family's
castle. Voice mail and answering machines are gate keepers
that prevent someone from having to speak with anyone they
don't wish to speak with.

However, a well-rehearsed answering machine message with
few details may entice potential clients to call you back.
Remember that your goal in cold calling is to actually
directly interact with someone in order to determine their
needs in buying or selling a property.

The method that has provided the highest percentage of call backs for my team has been to leave a message that simply states you want to talk to them in reference to either their home or your company. Do not waste your time asking on their machine whether or not they are planning to buy or sell. If they are, they are unlikely to call you back from a message.

The first method is to simply let them know that you're calling about their home. You are being completely honest, but they may hear the message to mean there is a problem or some situation they need to handle. This method has worked most effectively for us.

> *"Hi, Ms. Pratt. This is Dave Barry calling. I'm calling in reference to your home. Please call me back at your earliest convenience at 717-555-5555."*

The second method is to tell them you're calling in regard to your company. In this case the responses have been greater if you do not mention that you are *from* the company. The assumption made by many hearing the message is that there is an issue with the company, and they are interested in finding out what the problem may be.

> *"Hi, Mrs. Ivy. This is Greg Maguire calling. I'm calling in reference to Coldwell Banker Storm Breakers. Please call me back at your earliest convenience at 919-555-5555."*

Tracking your progress

When cold calling, I also suggest that you take the time to create some sort of *tally sheet* to track your progress. You'll find over time that you will become more creative and more successful in cold calling as you track which scripts work best in your market.

A tally sheet or tracking sheet would contain the following categories:

- The number of calls you made.
- The number of messages you left on voice mail or answering machines.
- The number of people you actually spoke with.
- The number of people who made an appointment to meet with you.
- The number of people who called you back from your voice mail message.

The creation of an elaborate tracking system is not critical when beginning a cold calling program. Too many agents get caught up in the details. The goal is to pick up the phone and find live prospects. However, tracking is very helpful in the long term in both improving your success ratio and in motivation when you can actually see the results of your efforts.

Door Knocking

Just as with cold calling, you should never discount the value of personal contact. Door knocking can actually be more effective than cold calling because people find it much more difficult to slam the door in the face of a salesperson, yet many people have no such compunction about hanging up on a salesperson.

Even so, some home owners will be rude and may let you know that they don't appreciate you knocking on their door.

That's a fact of life. There are grumpy people everywhere in the country, except possibly for a small rural area in southwest Utah. You need to shrug that off. Many agents use the *"mean people"* excuse for *not* door knocking. The truth is that you will find far more friendly people than unfriendly. Many of the country's top agents began their lucrative careers by door knocking.

With any program of personal contact, safety comes first. Make sure you visit neighborhoods you are familiar with. Carry a can of pepper-spray or another defensive spray. If a prospect that makes you uncomfortable invites you into the home, let them know you're only in the neighborhood for a few minutes, so you'd like to schedule a time to come back.

When planning a door knocking campaign, as with cold calling, start with a reason or objective for your visit. A reason for your visit might be to inform the neighbors of a recently sold home, of a recently listed home or of an open house.

Select a time when you believe more people will be at home in order to maximize your efficiency when walking a neighborhood. Try not to select a time which would upset the people you're visiting, such as the dinner hour.

Approaches to Door Knocking

One great method of door knocking is to inform neighbors of a home that you recently placed on the market for sale. There are three reasons this is effective. First, neighbors are naturally curious about what the value is of their home, and they partially base it on asking prices of other homes in the neighborhood.

Second, when one home goes for sale in a neighborhood, it gets the neighbors thinking of selling and moving up as well. You may be able to capitalize on that by offering a free analysis of what their home is worth.

Last, your door knocking script may be used to show that you are a very diligent, hard working Realtor trying to sell their neighbor's home. When the neighbor considers selling, he or she will remember that you went above and beyond simply putting a sign in the yard.

You may include language in your script that often a home is sold to a friend of one of the neighbors and do they know of anyone considering moving into the area. This language can lay the ground work for building a relationship with the neighborhood.

Agent: *"Hi. My name is Web Templeton and I'm with Action and Adventure Realty. I hate to bother you on such a beautiful Saturday, but I just listed your neighbor, Harlan Coben's house for sale at the end of the block. It's the beautiful two-story colonial with the white pillars. Anyway, very often buyers for homes are friends of other neighbors who admire the neighborhood. Who might you know that would be interested in living here in this great neighborhood?"*

Neighbor: *"No one I can think of right now."*

Agent: *"That's fine. May I give you my card in case you think of anyone who might like Mr. Coben's home?"*

Neighbor: *"Sure."*

Agent: *"Great. Here it is. Oh, by the way, when are you planning to move?"*

At the end of the conversation, you've been able to pass on your card to the neighbor and you've shown the neighbor that you work much harder than the average Realtor. Topping it off is a Columbo-style ending which usually catches the neighbor a bit off-guard and he or she may answer the question. *"Well, I'm planning to stay here until they carry me out in a box"* is one possible outcome. Another is, *"We plan to sell sometime in the Spring."* You now have a lead to follow up.

Some agents prefer a more direct approach. Using the same "just listed" technique, you may simply want to talk about property values and how the neighbor may be affected by the sale of your new listing.

Agent: *"Hi. My name is Dan Brown. I'm with Fortress Real Estate. I hate to bother you on a beautiful weekend like this one, but I wanted to let you know that I've just listed Anne Perry's home for sale around the corner on Downing Street. I'm don't know if you realize it, but the amount your neighbor's home sells for can affect the appraised value of your home. Were you aware of that?"*

Neighbor: *"I guess. What are they asking for the home?"*

Agent: *"It's currently listed at $429,900, which I personally feel is a very good price. We're getting a lot of activity on the home and I think it's going to go quickly. I'm hoping to find others in the neighborhood who might be considering selling as* *well. Do you know anyone else in the neighborhood who might be thinking of selling their home?"*

Neighbor: *"Not that I can think of."*

Agent: *"Okay. Please allow me to give you my business card. If you think of anyone, please give me a call. By the way, when are you planning to sell?"*

One of the reasons to first ask if the neighbor knows of anyone *else* thinking of selling is to take the pressure off them from answering about their own plans. Again, a Columbo-style question at the end of your interview is often more effective in determining the neighbor's ultimate plans.

Door Hangers

I'm generally hesitant to talk about door hangers when training new real estate agents. The reason is that if I mention anything remotely positive, agents sneak up to front doors and hang door hangers, and then run away without ever knocking on the door.

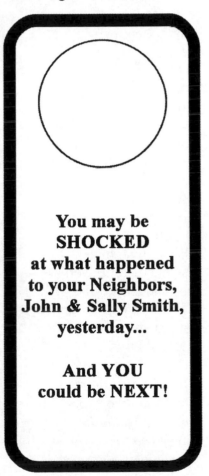

You may be SHOCKED at what happened to your Neighbors, John & Sally Smith, yesterday...

And YOU could be NEXT!

I believe door hangers can be a valuable tool when an owner is not home in a neighborhood you are canvassing. The likelihood that you will be back to the neighborhood soon is remote, so it's better to leave something behind that at least has a chance of making a difference.

As with postcard mailers, door hangers should have an eye catching headline that draws the viewer into reading the rest of the message. The compelling headline should be on the front of the hanger.

The back of the door hanger should have the information you want the person to read. Each door hanger should also have a compelling offer on the back, such as a free informational booklet, to attract them to contact you.

When canvassing apartments for buyers, a door hanger may be written about mortgage programs that are attractive to potential buyers.

A headline might read something like *"Your Landlord would like to Thank You for throwing your money away every*

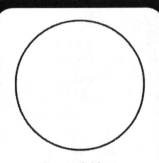

Your neighbors,
John & Sally Smith,
have decided to move to a
larger home. They selected
Bill Patterson
from Pat Riley Homes
to represent them in selling their
lovely 3 bedroom home.

If you know anyone who is
considering moving to the
neighborhood - please have
them call Bill at 919-555-5555.

And if you're considering
moving, don't do anything until
you get's Bill's free report on
Selling for Top Dollar.
Full of real estate insider secrets,
the report is absolutely free!

month in rent". The back of the card would outline how the tenant could own a home for around the same cost as they are paying in rent.

In any situation, however, I recommend knocking on the door prior to leaving anything behind. Ultimately you are far more likely to find a prospect and possibly get an appointment by actually speaking with someone rather than simply leaving a message behind.

Three Step Door Knocking System

One method of building business rapidly in a neighborhood is what I call the Three Step Door Knocking System. Remember that neighbors begin thinking about moving when they see others in the neighborhood move. In order to position yourself as the neighborhood Realtor and greatly increase your chances of being called for an interview, you should visit all the neighbors three times in a relatively short period of time. They will get to know you and think of you first when considering selling.

> TIP: If you don't have any listings of your own, ask others in the office if they'd mind you canvassing around one of their listings. Very few agents canvass and some may not mind you working the neighborhood.

The first time you knock on the door is when you first list the property. Ask them if they know of anyone considering moving into the area.

The second time you knock should be within two weeks of the first time. This time you should be inviting them and anyone they know to an open house you'll be holding at the new listing. You should have a flyer with you to give them about the open house. You may even ask them if they might post it at work.

Agent: *"Hi again, I don't know if you remember me, but I'm Pauly Shore with Hush Realty and I'm marketing Brian Tracy's home around the corner. We're having an open house this weekend on the property, and we're inviting everyone in the neighborhood to stop by and view their home. It's truly lovely. Also, I really need to get this home sold for them so they can move to their new home. If you wouldn't mind putting this up at your work place or giving a copy to anyone you know who may be moving, that would be wonderful."*

The third time canvassing is to let them know you sold the home, and you're wondering if they know anyone else who might be considering selling.

Agent: *"Hi again. It's Jimmy Kimmel from Striker Realty. As you may recall, I've been marketing Robert and Linda Harris' home for sale at the end of the block. I'm pleased to inform you that the home was sold, and for a very good price."*

Neighbor: *"That's great. What did it sell for?"*

Agent: *"I'm sorry, I'm not allowed to disclose that until the property settles. I'd be happy to call you once it closes and let you know the sales price."*

Neighbor: *"No. That's okay, I was just curious."*

Agent: *"Well, anyway, when we were marketing the home, many buyers came to see the property, and some are still looking for a home. Do you know anyone in the area that is considering making a move?"*

Performing the entire three step process will increase your exposure to the neighborhood and exponentially increase your likelihood for other listings in the neighborhood.

Building your database

While I'm covering door knocking, you should remember all the way back to Chapter 1. The goal of prospecting is not simply to find clients for the present, but also to build a database of potential clients you can contact over and over again. Building a sphere of influence database is one of the most powerful long term tools to your success in real estate.

Door knocking presents the perfect opportunity to ask if someone would allow you to keep in touch with them. You are already face to face and have introduced yourself, and you've explained the purpose of your visit. You can end your door knocking presentation by asking their permission to be included in your valuable mailers.

Agent: *"Thanks again for your time. By the way, from time to time, I send my friends and clients information on the real estate market. Would you be interested in receiving it?"*

This is a non-threatening approach to obtaining their permission to stay in touch. My experience is that most people will agree, and you'll be able to continually build your network.

Vacant Lot Owners

Many vacant lots or home sites across the country have been
inherited or have been purchased by individuals planning to
build their dream home, but for some reason never built it.
Others are investors who bought vacant land parcels in order
to develop them, but their plans changed before the
construction. You will also discover buyers and investors
who purchased land for speculation; simply to hold onto
until some future date. In all these situations, these property
owners are very good prospective sources of listings.

Search your local tax records for vacant land. Call the
owners and ask them if they're planning to build on the land
or if they're planning to sell the land.

> *"Hi, Mrs. Johnson? This is June Cleaver calling
> from Hometown Real Estate. I came across your
> property on Alberdeen Drive today while I was
> researching other properties. I was curious if you
> planned to build on that site or if you were planning
> to sell it?"*

A few years ago, I was asked to attend a meeting in Virginia.
On a whim, I looked up all the vacant land parcels in my
region that were owned by companies or individuals in
Virginia. I sent out a note to all of them announcing that I'd
"be in their area" for a meeting and if they were considering
selling their property in Pennsylvania, I'd love to meet with
them. I then followed up with phone calls. Ultimately, I
scheduled seven listing appointments all over the eastern part
of Virginia, and left for Virginia two days early. I listed four
of the properties in just over a day because the clients were
pleased that I could meet them in person.

Expired Listings Systems

Expired Listings are properties that have been on the market with a real estate broker for a period of time that failed to sell during their listing contract. These properties have been taken off the market by the owners, or their listing contract with their realtor has expired. In most areas of North America, expired listings can be found in the local Multiple Listing System.

Many of these properties are listed again with another real estate broker within days of the property being taken off the market. Most expired listings come back on the market within a year, unless seller's plans have changed or the seller finds they cannot sell the property for enough money to cover their move. Once a person or family decides to relocate, move up to a larger home, or move down to a smaller one, or simply gets an uncontrollable itch for new surroundings, they generally *do* move. Even if the owners take a few months off in between Realtors, they generally re-list at some point.

Calling or stopping by the home of an expired listing can be a quick method of building your personal listing inventory. Although the expired listing market *can* be a very lucrative source of business, it is one market where you will run into a lot of competition from other agencies and other agents.

There are two important reminders when working the expired market. First, take the time to create a game plan for how you're going to approach expired listings. As you work the expired market, you'll be able to "tweak" your methods or approach and improve them. Second, as with any other form of prospecting, make sure if you're going to target expired listings, that you do it consistently. Don't simply take a hit-or-miss approach by calling through the expired list once, or even once in a while and expect it to work. Consistency is the key to any long term success.

How do you find expired listings? On most multiple listing systems, simply run a search of properties that have status expired, with an expiration date of today or yesterday. You may choose to go back as far as a week. If you go back too far, however, chances are they've already listed with someone else, and you're wasting your time. You should contact the seller of an expired property the day that the property expires from the market.

The only deviation I have from this philosophy is to consider contacting old expired listings twice a year. First, just after the holiday season in January, some property sellers who chose not to re-list the prior year are beginning to consider testing the waters again. The second time period is about two weeks before the market gets hot. In many parts of the country, the spring market is when buyers come out to look at homes. This also leads many home sellers to place homes back on the market that were off for a period of time. If you contact older expired listings, you may hit them at *just* the right time.

The Seller's Perspective

As you consider your approach to the owner of an expired property, consider their mindset or frame of reference when you contact them. What is going through their mind is that they listed their home with a Realtor six months ago, and their expectation was that the home would sell too fast and they'd have to be out of the home too quickly. After all, they have the nicest home in the neighborhood. Everybody does.

They chose a Realtor who had a good reputation, or was from a reputable firm, and they haven't heard from that Realtor in the last four and a half months. These people are very upset. They are depressed. They're mad at all Realtors because we're all sales people, after all. We should be ranked up there with used cars; not just the used car salespeople, but the actual used cars. To complete their thought process, they don't understand why *you* didn't sell their home when it was on the markct. Obviously, the home was available on the multiple listing system. Why *wouldn't* you have sold it?

You are potentially walking into a situation where there are some very unhappy people who do not believe what Realtors' say, and they probably don't even realize that the house went off the market yet. They knew it was coming up at some point, but they haven't heard from their agent in so many months, and they haven't checked the date on the contract that they thought it was still available for sale.

Suddenly, out of the blue, this unhappy couple receives somewhere between 30 and 100 phone calls. This is not an exaggeration. Half of these callers will say exactly the same thing because they've been trained by Mike Ferry or Floyd Wickman[2]. Incidentally, I'm not criticizing either of these two exceptional trainers, I highly recommend going to see one or both, but they've been *so* successful that their words seem to be ingrained into every company in the country.

---

[2] Floyd Wickman is the creator of the highly successful Sweathogs training program, the SMART program and many others. His information can be viewed online at www.floydwickman.com

The day after the home expires, they'll get around 50 or more letters from Realtors all over the region. Most of the letters will say the exact same thing, because half of them will have been from the Craig Proctor system and the other half will simply print a letter out of the software program Top Producer. A dozen of the letters will be from agents claiming to be the very top selling agent in the whole area, and remember that the home owner is just getting out of a relationship with a Realtor they believe lied to them. Many of these letters will even contain bar graphs showing how their company outsells everyone else in the Eastern Hemisphere. How does an owner know what's true and what's not true? It's easier to believe we're all full of it.

My team at Century 21 Keim Realtors in Eastern Pennsylvania is composed of a number of highly trained and skilled brokers and agents. Because we have a successful group, several years ago we found that many agents were continually bumping into each other with the same approaches to expired listings, and they were frustrated. We spent a considerable amount of time putting together a series of different approaches to expired listings in order to attract different property sellers. In this text, we'll outline 5 of the approaches we used successfully.

Different individuals gravitate toward different messages. Some home owners will call back on a carefully handwritten note. Others will want a complete package of information before they'll call. Still others are attracted by something humorous or attention grabbing. We tried a variety of approaches and tested their effectiveness.

Each of these methods involves mailing or delivering something to the home owner. I need to be blunt here and explain that the best approach to prospecting is always direct contact. In other words, stopping by the home and introducing yourself in person is by *far* the most effective method of capturing expired listings. The second most effective is to have a phone conversation with the owner. Because I realize that most Realtors will never ever actually stop by a home unannounced, the methods included are alternatives to the direct approach.

There are two keys to getting the attention of the owner of an expired listing. The first key is to remember that you have to stand out above the crowd of agents who all send similar letters. It's all in the approach. You have to think outside the box and do something completely different than everybody else.

The second key is to look at the seller's needs from *their* perspective, not yours. Any time you're attacking any market, whether the market is bank foreclosure departments, relocation departments in major corporations, estate attorneys, or expired listings, you need to figure out what you can do to help them. What benefit do they need?

For expired listings, I actually have 2 suggestions for thinking from the owner's perspective. First, the home owner is unhappy with Realtors. They do not want to be tied into another six month contract. They do not want to get "stuck" with another bad experience with a house not selling, because they refuse to believe that the house didn't sell because it was priced too high. They believe the house didn't sell because of the Realtor's ineptitude and poor marketing skills. They are also mad at their prior Realtor for not calling them back. You can positively impact these sellers with a "Listing Cancellation Guarantee" that allows the seller to cancel your listing contract if they are unhappy with your service.

The other way you can positively impact this group is by "specializing" in their situation. You can send out a letter explaining that you are the neighborhood expert, the split level expert, the historic home expert, or the expert in handling market-challenged properties that didn't sell during their initial listing period.

Script for Calling Expired Listings

Your goal is to get an appointment, not to sell the owner on yourself or your company over the phone. Unless the owner is out of state, it is nearly impossible to get them to list their property over the phone. You need to identify yourself, confirm that the property is no longer for sale, and figure out a way to get the seller to meet you in person.

My approach has always been almost apologetic.

> *"Mr. Carrigan? I'm really sorry to bother you at home. I noticed that your home went off the market today. I realize you've probably had a dozen other calls already, but I service the area, and I was just wondering... were you still planning to sell the home?"*

There are several ways a home owner can react to this statement, and you need to be prepared for any of them. Some will tell you *"My phone has not stopped ringing. I wish you blood suckers would just leave me alone."* Others will be surprised. *"My home went off the market? No, it didn't."* Whatever their reaction, you need to keep them on the phone, build rapport with them, sympathize with their situation and look for a reason to meet with them. A strong technique to accomplish this is to end each comment you make with a question.

Sample Dialogue 1:

Agent: *"Mr. West? I'm really sorry to bother you at home. I noticed that your home went off the market today. I realize you've probably had a dozen other calls already, but I service the area, and I was just wondering... were you still planning to sell the home?"*

Client: *"My home went off the market? No, it didn't."*

Agent: *"I'm sorry. I didn't realize that you didn't know. When you list with a Realtor, the listing contract has a specific length. Your contract was apparently up and your home went off the MLS today. Didn't your agent tell you it was coming up to expire?"*

Client: *"No, they didn't."*

Agent: *"Wow, Mr. West. I'm really sorry. Are you still planning to move?"*

Client: *"You can call me Wally, and I'm not sure what I want to do now."*

Agent: *"If I may ask, where were you planning to move?"*

Client: *"The west coast of Florida. I'd like to retire and move somewhere warmer."*

Agent: *"I love Florida. I've helped a lot of clients over the years to move south. I'm just looking over your listing on the MLS and I'm really surprised that the home didn't sell during the listing period. Would you mind, I don't want to impose, but would you mind if I stopped by and looked at the home?"*

Client: *"We're not ready to hire another Realtor."*

Agent: *"That's no problem. Really, all I'd like to do is get an idea what may have happened. I can go over the market with you and give you my opinion of your home. I can try to figure out what went wrong, or why it didn't sell. Then, if you ever do decide to put the property on the market again, you'll have another opinion. Would you be free for me to stop by an evening this week? Or would during the day be better for you?"*

Sample Dialogue 2:

Agent: *"Mrs. Belldehoppen? I'm really sorry to bother you at home. I noticed that your home went off the market today. I realize you've probably had a dozen other calls already, but I service the area, and I was just wondering... were you still planning to sell the home?"*

Client: *"My phone has not stopped ringing. I really don't wish to talk to any more Realtors."*

Agent: *"I understand. I'd probably feel the same way. You put your home on the market, expecting it to sell quickly and something went wrong, and now you're probably being hounded by every other Realtor in the area."*

Client: *"Yes, I am."*

Agent: *"Do you have any idea why the home didn't sell?"*

Client: *"No, and I'm really very busy."*

Agent: *"I understand. I don't want to take much of your time, but you're in my market area and I've been looking at your listing information and it really looks like a beautiful home. Did your agent even advertise the property?"*

Client: *"I have no idea. I haven't heard from my agent in months."*

Agent: *"Wow, that's awful. Didn't they at least do some open houses or something?"*

Client: *"Just in the very beginning."*

Agent: *"Where were you planning to move?"*

Client: *"I'm staying in the same school district. We've just outgrown the house and we need more space."*

Agent: *"Well, you're certainly in a very good district. I've helped a lot of clients in the district over the past several years. Again, I'm really surprised your home didn't sell during the listing period. Would you mind, I don't want to impose, but would you mind if I stopped by and looked at the home?"*

Client: *"I'm really a very busy person."*

Agent: *"That's no problem. I just want to take a quick look. I may even be able to figure out what went wrong, or why it didn't sell. Then, if you ever do decide to put the property on the market again, you'll have another opinion. Would you be free for me to stop by an evening this week? Or would during the day be better for you?"*

Sample Dialogue 3:

Agent: *"Mrs. Leiderhosen? I'm really sorry to bother you at home. I noticed that your home went off the market today. I realize you've probably had a dozen other calls already, but I service the area, and I was just wondering... were you still planning to sell the home?"*

Client: *"Yes, but I'm going to be much more careful when I hire an agent this time. I plan to interview 3 or 4 different agents because I had a very bad experience with my last agent."*

Agent: *"I understand. If I were you, I'd do exactly the same thing. It never hurts to get several opinions on the pricing of a property and to hear different methods of marketing homes. If you're going to interview several agents, I'd really love to be one of those you interview. Would that be possible?"*

Client: *"That depends. What is your commission rate?"*

Agent: *"That's negotiable. We can certainly discuss it, and I'm open to your thoughts. When were you planning to conduct interviews?"*

Client: *"Early next week."*

Agent: *"That would work fine for me. If possible, would you consider interviewing me first?"*

Client: *"I guess."*

Agent: *"I work a little differently than most agents. My goals are to build a long term relationship with each of my clients. I do that by going above and beyond the norm when I'm marketing a home and delivering service. I always tell owners who are considering selling a property that they should select an agent based on the strength of their marketing and service. If you interview me first, you can measure other agent's marketing plans against mine."*

Client: *"That sounds good."*

Agent: *"Would an evening work better for you, or during the day?"*

Expired Listing System 1 – The Expired Package

As explained earlier in this section, there are two primary messages that owners of expired listings tend to respond to. First, they don't want to be tied down with another agent who doesn't provide them service. So you need to convince them that you will provide that service.

One way to *show* the seller that you mean what you say about service is to offer the seller a method to hold you accountable. Put the control into their hands. You can provide the seller with an "Listing Cancellation Guarantee" or "Fire Me Guarantee", where you guarantee if the seller is unhappy with your service, they can cancel the listing. This is a hard pill for most agents to swallow, because they believe every listing will cancel. The truth is that some will. The further truth is that you will list far more homes *because* you offer proof of your service than you will lose.

The second message that an expired listing will respond to is that you specifically work in their market, know their type of home or are a specialist for their type of property. Everyone loves a specialist who really understands their particular needs. Remember that the home seller probably still believes that the price wasn't really an issue. The main problem, in their mind, is that the prior Realtor didn't understand how to market the property properly, so they're looking for someone who can show them a "different" way to market.

The approach I used to "stand out" from the vast majority of Realtors was to mail out a large package, rather than a #10 envelope with a letter. The package cost a lot more to put together and to mail than a simple letter, but I got a far greater response from the package than I did from any letter I ever sent.

The package was a 9 x 12 envelope stuffed with information. The information inside included a letter highlighting why my team and I were different than most real estate agents, an explanation of our guarantees, including a release of listing if they were unhappy with our service and a guarantee of feedback and weekly calls, and a brief description of our marketing. The rest of the package was filled with samples.

We created a nice *"Listing Cancellation Guarantee"* certificate called the *"Easy Cancellation Policy"* that allowed the home owner to see our guarantee more than once. We also included a page just dedicated to our guarantees, a photo page of our team and their job descriptions, a sample of our full color home flyers, and a 12 page booklet we wrote on "why some homes don't sell".

These clients are starved for information. How could it be that *their* home didn't sell, while the ugly one down the street with the pale green shutters sold in only 7 days? It must be that no one knew their home was for sale. Our booklet explained the 3 primary reasons a home doesn't sell: marketing, staging and pricing. It also gave the owner who read the booklet the opportunity to call us, with no obligation, for an analysis to figure out which of the reasons may have impacted the home's sale when it was on the market the first time.

You can even create several different packages that are targeted at specific types of properties. One package could be created for condos and townhomes with a sample flyer of each. One package could be created for luxury properties, average homes, historic homes, farms, vacant land, or any other type you can think of.

Expired Listing System 2 – Morning Delivery

Not wanting to duplicate my efforts, other agents in our company attempted completely different approaches that would stand out from the crowd. One method was developed by Tim Mahon and Wayne Talaber. They felt that if they could be the very first people to talk to the owner about their situation, before the seller received 50 calls and 35 letters, they'd be far more likely to get the listing.

The problem was that in order to be first, an agent would probably have to call the seller of an expired listing or stop by their home at 6 am to beat all the other agents to the punch. Neither agent believed they would get a good reception from the potential listing at 6 in the morning.

They came up with an alternative plan. Most families are dual income and most home sellers leave for work in the morning and wouldn't even know that a Realtor had called until they returned home that evening and played back their full answering machine or voice mail. Further, when one of our agents *was* the first Realtor to speak with an expired listing, they often found the home owner had no idea the home was going off the market *that particular day*. They hadn't spoken with their agent in a significant period of time, so they weren't aware the expiration date was coming up.

Wayne was already an early-bird, so he decided he would go to the office before 5 in the morning and pull off a copy of the daily expired list. This method, by the way, is not for the night owl or those of you who have trouble getting out of bed before 10.

In order to get to the client before everyone else in the real estate industry, between 5 am and 6 am, Wayne and Tim would go to the homes of expired listings and hang a plastic bag on the front door with information in the bag. The plastic bags are very similar to those used to deliver newspapers. Since the bags were hung on the front door knob, the owner would hopefully see the bag when he or she came out in the morning to get the paper or to leave for work.

Inside, Wayne and Tim had a package of information about their services. Most importantly, the clear plastic bag allowed them to face the headline of their message out, so anyone picking up the bag could easily read the note. I always believe that 90% of the message is in the headline. If you don't believe it, check out the Presidential elections. Their headline read *"Do you know your home is no longer on the market for sale??"* This headline actually took up 1/3 of the paper so it would be clearly readable through the plastic bag.

The home owner would bring the bag into the home in the morning, or take the bag with them to work. They would see the headline and open the package because the headline surprised them. The brief letter under the note explained that homes are placed on the market in the MLS for a period of time, and that period of time had expired with their current Realtor. That means the home was no longer available in the multiple listing system.

In over a hundred cases, the home owner would call Wayne or Tim from work to ask about the letter. These agents become the first contact with the expired home's owner, making them far more likely to get an appointment.

"Tim, I found your note on my door this morning. It says that my home's not on the market for sale anymore. I don't understand. What do you mean it expired?" Again, owners don't necessarily know our lingo. Tim or Wayne would explain to the property owner that his or her contract ended with their Realtor.

Did You Know Your Home
Is No Longer On The Market For Sale?

The listing agreement with your current Realtor has expired and your home was taken off the Multiple Listing System today.

Very often, when a home is taken off the MLS, dozens of Real Estate agents call the owner and mail literature to the owner making the owner all sorts of promises in order to get you to list with them.

I believe I'm a bit different than other Realtors in the area. For example, I'm so sure of my service that I offer a guarantee that if you are unhappy with my service at any time… you can fire me. You can cancel the listing with no questions asked. I call this my "Listing Cancellation Guarantee."

What I *would* like is to have the opportunity to spend a few moments with you and find out what your plans and needs are. Then I can determine if and how I can help you.

Please call me at 000-000-0000

An easy question from our agents would *"Were you happy with the service your current Realtor gave you?"* The answer is almost always "No". The owner didn't even realize the home had expired, and probably hadn't heard from the agent in four or five months. Because there was less hostility from the owner than if Tim or Wayne had been the 27th phone call to the owner, they could also ask *"Are you still planning to sell the home, or are you planning to stay?"*

Expired Listing System 3 – Felt Tip Note Cards

Another agent with our firm, Rob, had a little bit different approach to the same problem. Ultimately, what the home owner wants is to get the property sold. What we, as Realtors, want is to get an appointment to meet with the home owner in order to show them our marketing and servicing plan and why our plan is better than what they had previously.

Rob's method was based on the fact that many sellers are grasping at anyone who may be interested in purchasing their home *now* rather than waiting for another full marketing cycle with another Realtor. I'm not suggesting what Rob did was right or wrong, just that it was very effective in getting home sellers to call *him*, rather than the other way around.

Rob purchased plain white 4" x 6" or larger postcards. He used a larger than typical postcard in order to stand out in the mail. He then took a felt tip pen and hand wrote, *"Dear _____, I'm wondering if you would consider selling your home to one of my buyers. Please call me, Rob"*.

Next, he would go to the local Kinko's or print shop and have a thousand of these cards printed. Each day, Rob would pull the expired list and complete each card. Using the same felt tip marker, he would fill in the *"Dear _____"* with the owner's first name, *"Dear Jim"*. On the other side he'd write Jim Smith, 123 Main Street, Mertztown, Pennsylvania, and send it out. People would make the assumption that Rob had a buyer interested in their house and they would call him.

Dear ___ ,

I'm wondering if you would consider selling your home to one of my buyers.

Please call me,

Rob

Again, I'm not suggesting this is a good approach or a bad approach, but it worked very effectively for Rob. There are two ways to look at the real estate industry. One way is that we are all here to make a living, and if we can do that without being illegal or unethical, then a little misleading or misdirection is not terrible if the end result is that the seller sells his or her home and the agent gets paid for some hard work.

The second way to look at the real estate industry, which is typically my thought process, is that we are here to provide a service to the community. Understand that I'd like to be paid for that service, my experience, my expertise, and my negotiating ability, but I'm still providing a valuable service. I don't want people sitting around at a party telling their friends how I misled them. I'd rather not have that piece of business if that's the way I would have to work, although I respect methods that attain a successful end result.

I was in a training course some years ago listening to super trainer Floyd Wickman explain that he certainly *did* use techniques, objection handling tactics and salesmanship to get buyers and sellers to work with him, but clients loved him for it. His end result was that he delivered more than the competitors did for his clients, and in some cases, he had to use techniques to do it. My favorite line from Floyd is "*I never got a Christmas card from a prospect, only those that I techniqued.*"

Owners of expired listings that received Rob's card would call and ask:

Client: "*Do you have a buyer for my home?*"

Rob's response was fairly simple:

Agent: "*I don't know, I haven't seen it yet, but I'm working with a lot of buyers. I'm hoping that one of them will like your house. I saw it went off the market, and it looked like a beautiful home. I can't believe it expired, and I do have a lot of buyers I'm working with*".

Client: "*Well, why didn't you sell it when it was on the market?*"

Agent: "*Well, you know at Century 21 Keim, we try to sell our own listings first. That's what our home sellers hire us to do, and it's what's fair to our sellers. Anyway, I wouldn't mind stopping out, at least taking a walk through your house. That way I can tell you whether or not it will work for one of my buyers*".

Once you've managed to get in the door and meet with the home owner in person, you can use a surprised approach. "Wow, this is really a nice home. I'm surprised it didn't sell." Always remember to be honest, however. Do not say how nice the home is if there really are no redeeming qualities about it. Next, build rapport and begin a conversation with the goal to lead into talking about marketing the home and what your firm might do that would be a little different than other companies. This approach was very effective.

Incidentally, our firm dominated the expired listing market for quite a period of time. Each of the approaches outlined in this section work, and each is just as effective as the others. We seldom overlapped with listing appointments, even though we went after the same customers. Some owners responded to the morning delivery. Others responded to the hand written post card and still others found the package was most interesting.

Expired Listing System 4 – Needle-in-a-Haystack Boxes

At a real estate workshop in the late 1990's, I met Tom Cooke, a Re/Max agent who worked as a team with his wife Sally in Toronto. He told me about a method that he or one of the other agents he was associated with used on expired listings. Again, I don't want to plagiarize his method, but we've been using a similar method now on and off for well over ten years. We call it the needle-in-a-haystack box.

In Pennsylvania, it's relatively easy to find hay. We would fill a small box with hay. Next we would buy a package of those large plastic needles that are sold at Wal-Mart, Target and other fine retailers. We'd then punch a hole in our team business card and tie the needle to our card with a piece of yarn. We buried the needle in the… you guessed it, hay, and placed our card on top. Last, we would close and seal the box, writing across the top *"Finding a Great Real Estate Team is like finding a Needle in a Hay Stack"*.

Remember that creativity sells like nothing else! Our goal is to stand out from the crowd. Most recently, agents Bonnie Smith and Marlene Moser from our firm have used this technique to begin building a strong listing inventory. They would leave these boxes on the door step of expired listings (or for sale by owners).

Putting these boxes together takes time, patience and a little bit of money. But the boxes catch a lot of attention and prove unequivocally that the team leaving the box approaches marketing much differently than any other Realtor the sellers might meet.

The box, picture to the right, has a note on top *"Finding the right Realtors is like finding a needle in the haystack."*

The box is filled with hay with the agent's business card prominently featured on top.

The card is tied to an inexpensive plastic needle.

Expired Listing System 5 – Crumpled Letters

We have utilized several other unique approaches that have worked as well. Our "Crumpled Letter Campaign" involved visually showing the property owner that we understand marketing and how to make ourselves stand out, which means we'll be more likely to make their home stand out.

We would print across the top of the letter *"For your convenience, we have pre-crumpled this letter."* Remember that the headline is critically important in any marketing piece you send to potential clients. The headline is what entices the prospect to actually read your message.

For your convenience, this letter has been Pre-Crumpled

The listing agreement with your current Realtor has expired and your home was taken off the Multiple Listing System today. By the time you read this letter, I'm certain that you've heard from dozens of Real Estate agents claiming to be the best in the marketplace and making all sorts of promises in order to get you to list with them.

I believe I'm a bit different than other Realtors in the area. What you need to sell your property is someone who understands how to market, or someone who understands how to make herself and her homes for sale "stand out" from all the competition. I'm the person to do that for you.

In addition to my marketing expertise, I offer a guarantee that if you are unhappy with my service at any time... you can fire me. You can cancel the listing with no questions asked. I call this my "Listing Cancellation Guarantee."

What I *would* like is to have the opportunity to spend a few moments with you and find out what your plans and needs are. Then I can determine if and how I can help you.

Please call me at 000-000-0000

In the letter itself, we would include language explaining why our service and marketing is a little different than the typical agent in the marketplace. The next step is to take the letter in your hands and crumple it into a ball. Once crumpled, flatten the letter again, and fold it so that the headline is immediately visible when the prospect opens the envelope.

We've found that expired property owners and for sale by owners are more likely to open the letter because it "feels" different than most of the letters they receive, and we've hand written their name and address on the outside. Hand written addresses are far more likely to be opened than printed addresses. Also, letters with stamps on them, instead of postage meter stamping, are also more likely to be opened.

For Sale By Owners

"For Sale By Owners" or FSBOs are obviously those people who choose to try selling their home without the advantages of having a professional Realtor working with them. There are three primary reasons that some home sellers attempt to sell on their own.

The first and most obvious reason is that they are trying to save the commission. The second reason is that they want control over the transaction and they feel out of control letting an agent handle the details. There is a third possibility as well. They may be trying to hide something from prospective buyers and you, as a professional, may prevent that from happening.

Those home sellers who try selling themselves are a great source of listings because, historically, most of them end up listing with a real estate agent. Despite this, they are very often the most challenging group to attempt to list.

If you, for example, were not a successful professional Realtor and you planned to sell your home, you might believe that an agent does nothing other than a bit of advertising in the newspaper and homes magazines. That 5 or 6% commission is a huge chunk of your potential savings. Wouldn't you at least try to sell on your own first? After all, you have the nicest home in the neighborhood, and you're pretty sure that *someone* out there will buy your home within a few days of advertising, right?

This is typical of many *"For Sale by Owners"*. They test the waters prior to listing with a Realtor because they want to save thousands of dollars.

In order to successfully list *"For Sale by Owners"*, you must understand their perspective and you must move slowly. Although most surveys indicate that between 70% and 90% of FSBOs eventually list their homes, most of these property owners *believe* they will be able to sell on their own. Rushing in to tell them about your services and why they will never sell on their own is a recipe for failure. Instead, you need to find a way to help them that is non-threatening.

The Reason 'For Sale By Owners' Fail

While it's true that some home sellers are able to sell their homes for top dollar by themselves, the vast majority end up listing with Realtors or settling for a lower-than-average price for their type of home in their area.

There are several reasons this happens. First, home sellers who try selling on their own don't have access to the same number of buyers that Realtors do. If you want to sell any product, whether it is a home, a toothbrush or a DVD, to obtain the highest price, you need to get the product in front of the most customers possible.

For example, if you created a product, like this book, and tried selling it on your own directly to consumers, you wouldn't have to pay the distribution warehouse, and you wouldn't have to pay Barnes & Noble, Borders or Amazon to sell it. Therefore, the theory goes, you'd make 4 or 5 times as much on each book if you simply sold it directly to the customer and bypassed the middle man and the retailers.

The problem with that kind of thinking is that most buyers looking for books shop online at Amazon or stop by their local Barnes & Noble or Borders. We're far more likely to sell our product if our product is available in the places that buyers shop.

Think about where buyers for your listings come from. Most homes sell through the multiple listing systems, which sellers can't utilize without a Realtor. Most direct home buyers that come to us first shop on the Internet, on major sites like Realtor.com, Century21.com, Homes.com, Remax.com and Yahoo Real Estate. Again, sellers without agents can't get their homes listed in these places without hiring an agent. The next most used media might be homes magazines and so on.

Sellers who choose the route of *"For Sale by Owner"* are typically limited to a sign, an ad in the newspaper and a listing on FSBO web sites. We all know that the newspapers are not the best source of leads for our listings in most parts of the country, and FSBO web sites get far fewer hits than the big guns like Realtor.com because buyers want access to *all* the listings, not just a select few.

One caveat, however, is that during a very hot market, when few homes are on the market, buyers *will* seek out any possible homes for sale.

The second reason private sellers don't get top dollar is that buyers realize the seller doesn't have to pay the commission to a Realtor, so the buyer automatically expects it to come off the list price. I can't tell you how often a buyer has told me, *"Well, I'm buying this home directly because I'm saving the commission."*

Those buyers in the marketplace searching through the private sale ads are working a little harder to find a deal than those who simply call a Realtor. They realize that FSBO sellers are not paying a commission, so they expect the seller to reduce their price by at least the price of the commission.

The third reason that *"For Sale by Owners"* often sell for less is that many buyers won't purchase a home privately without an agent. As I write this chapter, I'm at a Century 21 convention in Orlando, Florida. The keynote speaker is noted author and television personality Suzy Ormond. While in Orlando, she spoke with one of the bellhops who said he had purchased a home in the last two years directly from a seller. *"I'd never do it again,"* he said.

Buyers have to arrange for their own financing, pay an attorney to write an offer, find a title or escrow company and a home inspector, and handle all the details of the transaction themselves. On top of that, they worry about making a mistake that could cost them thousands of dollars. What if the seller is hiding something? Who will protect them?

Even though these are all valid reasons that *"For Sale by Owners"* typically sell for less than homes listed with a Realtor or end up listing with a Realtor despite all their efforts, you will usually fail in your attempt to list their home if you approach the seller with a direct explanation of their challenges. People believe what they want to believe, and they believe that you will say *anything* to get your 5, 6 or 7%. Therefore, you must approach them with a benefit that is honest and will help you to build a relationship with them, so that when they decide they need the services of a professional Realtor, they will call you.

Once you've approached the *"For Sale by Owner"* with a benefit, you need to stay in contact with that seller. Most private sellers only attempt to sell on their own for 3 to 5 weeks. That's not a long period of time. You'll need to contact them at least weekly, and preferably twice a week until they are ready to list. You'll also need reasons to contact them regularly that are not offensive or *pushy*.

For Sale By Owner System 1: Relocation

When someone is selling a home, they are most often moving to another home. They may be selling to relocate out of the area, or they may be selling to move to a bigger home in the same town. Certainly, there are people who try selling a property on their own that is a rental property, or that may be an estate or second home, but the vast majority of FSBOs are selling primary residences to move to another primary residence.

These home owners may try to save the commission by selling on their own, but may be very willing to have an agent work with them to *find* the perfect home. The goal of this technique is to introduce yourself as someone who can either assist them in purchasing their new home, or assist them by referring them to the *best* agent in another area and collecting a referral fee.

The secondary goal is in listing the home at a later date, if it doesn't sell *"by owner"*. If you become their agent on the buying end, you are far more likely to be the person they use to sell their home.

Whenever I speak with a *"For Sale by Owner"*, I always begin by telling them I am *not* calling to try to get them to list their home. As soon as you say your company name, they will be wary. You need to put them at ease as quickly as possible. Next follow up with an explanation of how you help people to find the perfect home. Sometimes that home is local, and sometimes that home is across the country.

The dialogue should go something like this:

Agent: *"Hi. Is this the owner of the property listed for sale in the newspaper?"*

Owner: *"Yes."*

Agent: *"Before I say anything else, I want to let you know that I am a Realtor, but I am not calling to try to list your home. My name is Alice Beckwith and I'm with*

*Century 21 Your Home Matters here in Feasterville.
Again, I'm not calling to try to list your home. What
I do is try to help people find the perfect property,
whether they stay local or move out of state. Since
you're selling your home, I was wondering where you
were moving to?"*

Owner: *"I'm planning to buy a larger home in the area. I'd
like to buy new construction."*

Agent: *"That's great. Do you have an agent working with
you to assist you in your purchase?"*

Owner: *"No, but I thought I'd go directly to the builders in
the area because I'll get a better deal."*

Agent: *"Actually, a lot of buyers think that. The truth is that
builders in the area generally charge you the same
amount whether you bring an agent or not. In fact, if
the builder is using a real estate firm to market their
properties, that agent represents the best interests of
the builder's – not yours. Bringing in a buyer's
agent to represent you not only costs you absolutely
nothing, but may help you to negotiate a better deal."*

Owner: *"I didn't know that."*

Agent: *"Most people don't. I'd love to stop by and spend a
few minutes with you discussing how I can help you
in finding the perfect new construction home and get
the best possible deal for you. Would it be possible
for me to stop by an evening this week? Or would it
be better if I stopped by on the weekend?"*

You may find that the seller is planning to move out of the area or across the country:

Agent: "*...What I do is try to help people find the perfect property, whether they stay local or move out of state. Since you're selling your home, I was wondering where you were moving to?*"

Owner:"*I'm taking a job transfer to Saint Charles, Missouri, so I'm not sure you can help me.*"

Agent: "*Wow, that's a beautiful area. It's near Saint Louis, right?*"

Owner:"*Yes, it is.*"

Agent: "*Do you have an agent you're working with in Saint Charles currently?*"

Owner:"*Not yet. I've been looking at listings online, but I didn't think I'd get serious until I have some offers on my home.*"

Agent: "*That's a good idea. I'm actually part of one of the country's largest relocation networks. I can research the market in Saint Charles and try to find you the best one or two agents that can handle your move. I would make sure that no one pressures you, but also make sure that they send you good information to help you find the right home in the perfect location. Too many buyers pick an agent off the Internet and get stuck with someone that doesn't have their best interests at heart. Would you mind if I did a little research using our relocation network to find you a dynamite agent who will work in your best interest?*"

Owner:"*I guess not.*"

Agent: "*Great. Let me ask you a few questions, just to understand what you're looking for in Missouri. What type of home would be perfect for you?*"

The only downside to this approach is that sometimes the "*For Sale by Owner*" has already found a home, or they are not planning to purchase again. This approach makes it difficult for you to recover and ask to see the home, because you've told them your purpose is to assist them in finding a new home.

One method of recovering is to mention that you're working with many other buyers as well:

Agent: "*Before I say anything else, I want to let you know that I am a Realtor, but I am not calling to try to list your home. My name is Alex Ross and I'm with Century 21 Keim Realtors here in Quakertown. Again, I'm not calling to try to list your home. What I do is try to help people find the perfect property, whether they stay local or move out of state. Since you're selling your home, I was wondering where you were moving to?*"

Owner:"*I'm staying in the area, but I've already purchased another home. I'm just waiting to settle on that one when this home sells.*"

Agent: "*That's great. Where is your new home?*"

Owner:"*On Overlook in the Stonesthrow neighborhood.*"

Agent: *"That's a great area. <pause> Would you be obligated to purchase that home even if your current home doesn't sell?"*

Owner: *"Oh, I don't think that will be a problem. My home is absolutely beautiful, and it's priced right."*

Agent: *"It sounded nice in the ad. Let me ask you another question. I'm working with a lot of other buyers at the moment. If I had a buyer that was looking for a home like yours, would you let me show it?"*

Owner: *"I don't want to pay a commission. That's why I'm selling myself."*

Agent: *"I understand that, and I'd try to build the commission into the purchase price. But if I had a buyer, would you let me show it?"*

Owner: *"I guess it wouldn't hurt."*

Agent: *"That sounds great. Would you mind if I stopped over and took a quick walk through, so I know what it looks like and can describe it to the buyer's I'm working with?"*

Keep in mind that any time you're speaking with a *"For Sale by Owner"* on the phone, your goal is to meet with the person face to face. The first agent who meets the prospective clients in person is generally the most likely to list the property, should the seller need assistance.

After a few weeks of working with *"For Sale by Owners"*, you'll also find that you'll have more success getting in the door if you are one of the very first agents to call them.

Once you've made it in the door, with any of the *"For Sale by Owner"* approaches, you'll need to lay out a strong follow-up program so that you stay in touch with them over the typical 3 to 5 weeks they attempt to sell on their own. Keep in mind that during this time frame, they'll continue to receive calls from other agents. You don't want to be displaced in the owner's mind by someone else.

Working with the owner as a buyer is a strong approach because it gives you the benefit of immediately sending listings, and then calling within a few days to see if any of the listings were ones the seller wants to view. You can continue sending listings and following up with phone calls without the worry of asking them to list. During this period, you may also ask how the sale of their home is going. If they like you as a buyer's agent, they'll be more likely to open up about their challenges.

If the seller is moving out of the area, you can create several contacts by first sending the seller a Thank You note, then contacting an agent or two in the area where the seller is relocating. Call the seller and let them know that you've found one or two great agents and that you've given them the seller's information. Follow up with the seller two or three days later to make sure they heard from those agents. Again, your primary goal is to maintain consistent contact.

For Sale By Owner System 2: I have a buyer

Similar to one of the approaches to Expired Listings, you can call with the purpose of explaining that you are a successful agent working with several buyers that are looking in the area. You simply want to determine if this particular owner would consider paying a partial commission if you brought them a buyer.

As with the prior approach, you want to assure the owner that you are not trying to list the home, at this point, because you don't want them to *shut down* and ignore everything else you say.

A sample dialogue would be:

Agent: *"Hi. Is this the owner of the property listed for sale in the newspaper?"*

Owner: *"Yes."*

Agent: *"Before I say anything else, I want to let you know that I am a Realtor, but I am not calling to try to list your home. My name is Maggie Alagoria and I'm with The Undertaker Realty here in Atlanta. Again, I'm not calling to try to list your home. However, I do work in the neighborhood and I have a number of buyers looking for homes right now. I was wondering if you would pay a commission if I brought you a buyer for your home?"*

Owner: *"Do you have a buyer for my home?"*

Agent: *"I don't know, I haven't seen it yet, but I'm working with a lot of buyers. I'm hoping that one of them will like your house. From the ad in the paper, it looks like a great property and I do have some serious buyers. Would you be willing to pay a fee if I brought you a buyer?"*

Owner: *"What kind of fee are you talking about?"*

Agent: *"Well, that can be negotiable and I'll try to build my fee into the price, but typically I am paid ½ the commission on a normal sale if another agent has the listing. Commissions range from X to Y, so I usually charge a fee for bringing a buyer between ½ X and ½ Y. Would that be acceptable?"*

Owner:*"I guess that doesn't sound too bad."*

Agent: *"Great! I'd like to stop out, if possible, and take a quick walk through the home so I can describe it to my buyers. What day works best for you? I'm free on Thursday evening, Friday morning and again on Saturday morning. What would be best?"*

For Sale By Owner System 3: Mortgage Co-Conspirator

A third method for approaching *"For Sale By Owners"* is to work with a mortgage originator or mortgage officer who can contact the owner because the owner may need financing for their new home, and certainly the buyers of their home will need financing. If and when the owner begins leaning toward the need for a Realtor, the mortgage originator can provide a third-party endorsement to you as the *best* agent the seller can use.

This approach requires you to enlist the aid of a mortgage officer who doesn't mind making some phone calls. If you're already giving your mortgage business to a particular person, you might suggest that they are likely to get mortgage leads out of this, and that you'll happily guarantee all of the future business you possibly can to this mortgage person.

The mortgage originator may even walk through the home to give the owners some advice, and then suggest they get a market analysis and some staging advice from an expert. *"I know this great agent, Carolyn, from Flying Eagle Real Estate who I'm sure would do a market analysis at no charge and she wouldn't pressure you to list. Should I give her a call?"*

A sample dialogue might be:

Mtg Broker: *"Hi, is this the owner of the property listed for sale in today's paper?"*

Owner: *"Yes, it is."*

Mtg Broker: *"Hi. My name is Rachel and I'm with Bank of Your Town. I'm not a Realtor, so don't worry. I'm just calling because I saw your ad and I was wondering... when you have buyers look at your home, do you have a good mortgage broker who can help qualify them to purchase your home?"*

Owner: *"Uh, no."*

Mtg Broker: *"Most people don't. It's so critical to make sure buyers qualify before taking the home off the market. What I can do for you is this; I can prepare a closing cost estimate on your home for potential buyers and prepare a flyer on your home that lays out several different mortgage programs and how much your home would be monthly for buyers. These flyers usually really help buyers to make up their*

> minds. *All I'd want in return is for you to refer them to me if they need a good mortgage company. Does that sound like a fair trade?"*

Owner: *"Yes, it does."*

Mtg Broker: *"Great. What I normally do is stop by for a few minutes and get some information and maybe borrow a few photos from you for the brochure. Then I can get it together in a day or so. Are you free during the day, or would the evening work better?"*

The mortgage broker can then lead into financing for the seller to purchase their new home as well. This approach is very powerful because the mortgage broker's contact of the owner is not viewed with the same fear a Realtors contact is, and further, the mortgage broker gives that all-important, third-party endorsement to the agent.

For Sale By Owner System 4: FSBO Survival Pack

One of the classic methods of approaching *"For Sale By Owners"* is to give them something of value. Put together a binder with much of the information the owner needs to sell their home, including a sales contract, buyer qualification form and perhaps a copy of the book *"How to Sell Your Home in Any Market,"* available in stores everywhere!

The difficulty I always encounter when teaching this technique is that agents believe they can simply mail the package to a *"For Sale by Owner"* or mail a letter suggesting they get a copy, without ever calling the property owner. In our tests, we've found agents are nine times more likely to list a *"For Sale by Owner"* if they meet the owner face to face. You will not meet them face to face by mailing something to them. You need to call, possibly follow up with a Thank You note and find a way to meet them.

A sample dialogue might be:

Agent: *"Hi. Is this the owner of the property listed for sale in the newspaper?"*

Owner: *"Yes."*

Agent: *"Before I say anything else, I want to let you know that I am a Realtor, but I am not calling to try to list your home today. My name is William Talltree and I'm with Lumberjack Realty here in the Great Lakes area. What I'd like to offer you is a fair trade. I'd like to drop off a full package of all the information and forms you might need to sell your home, including a blank Sales Contract, information on how a buyer might finance your home, and 20 more legal documents you may need to put a sale together. I'll also include some tips and techniques on how to stage a home. There's no charge and no obligation. There are 2 reasons I do this with home sellers who are selling on their own. First, you may find at some point that you want to hire an agent. If you do, I'd like the opportunity to be one of those you interview. Second, if you are able to sell on your own, I'm hoping that you'll be so impressed with the information I give you that you'll refer me to any of your family or friends who don't want to try selling on their own. Does that sound like a fair trade?"*

Whew, that is a mouth full, but it's also a strong approach to get in the door to meet them. They may respond that they're planning to use an attorney. That's okay. It still helps to understand what inspections, contingencies and conditions are typically put into any agreement between a buyer and seller.

Our FSBO Survival Packages include:

- A blank Sales Contract.
- A Seller's Property Disclosure Form.
- A blank Buyer's Financial Statement.
- Any contingency addendums found in your area
- A booklet that outlines the sales process including home staging, showing techniques, an explanation of the financing process, an outline of inspections and an outline of the escrow process or title insurance process. An alternative is a copy of the book "*How to Sell Your Home in Any Market*".
- An Open House Sign-in Sheet
- A list of local home inspectors.
- A list of local escrow companies or title insurance companies (depending on your state).
- A Repair Checklist
- 20 Questions to ask any agent before signing a listing.

For Sale By Owner System 5: The Honest Approach

The truth is that many of you would rather take a simple direct approach. When you're taking a direct approach, please keep in mind that many *"For Sale by Owners"* will tell you that they don't want to hear from you again. Your best method of meeting them might be a stealth tactic like the Relocation Approach or the Mortgage Co-Conspirator Approach.

A simple approach is to explain that you specialize in homes in the area, and you'd like to introduce yourself. Perhaps they'll sell their home on their own, and perhaps they won't. In either case, you'd like to be a source of information and experience for them if they have any questions.

If they decide to select a professional Realtor, you'd like to have the opportunity to interview. A dialogue might be:

Agent: *"Hi. Is this the owner of the property listed for sale in the newspaper?"*

Owner: *"Yes."*

Agent: *"Before I say anything else, I want to let you know up front that I am a Realtor. My name is Bruce Wayne and I'm with Sign of the Bat Real Estate here in Gotham. I truly respect your desire to sell your home on your own, and I promise not to bother you. I specialize in homes in this area, and I just wanted to make sure it's okay for me to drop off some information on myself and my team."*

Owner: *"I don't need an agent. I plan to sell the home on my own."*

Agent: *"That's no problem. I always feel that if I introduce myself to many of the individuals who try selling homes on their own, some of them may find, over time, that they want to move more quickly. Your circumstances may change and you may decide to interview agents. I just want to be included if you decide to interview. So, would you mind if I dropped off some literature about my team?"*

Other Short Term Prospecting Methods

There are literally dozens of methods to finding immediate business. Every time you drive by a vacant lot, you're driving by a potential listing for sale. Each time you read an article stating that a company has expansion plans, you have someone to contact that may be relocating people into your market area.

Any companies looking to expand are good targets. You need to start making contacts and building your book of business.

I once read about a Real Estate firm that had 25 agents and 25 telephones, but no desks. When agents worked in the office, they would have to stand. The broker claimed it was a very effective strategy because he wanted the agents out on the streets actually knocking on doors and doing something. I'm not sure how long I'd be able to maintain a staff if they had no place to sit down, but the story indicates the importance of getting out there and meeting people because that's where your business really is. This is a people business. This is a relationship business. This is relationship game and you have to meet people.

Chapter 8: Other Long Term Prospecting Methods

Farming for Business

The most commonly discussed long-term method of prospecting is farming. A farm can be a geographic area, such as a particular neighborhood or area around a particular school, or it can be a property type, such as historic homes, farms, vacant lots, or town homes. The downside to farming is that you will need to contact the same group over and over until they begin to recognize you. It may take a year to eighteen months to actually see any results from your work. The upside to farming is that once you become known as the specialist in that area or property type, it becomes very difficult for another Realtor to unseat you.

For example, as I mentioned earlier in this book, one of my primary specialties was horse farms. I had chosen that type of property as one that I thought was being ignored by the established real estate brokers. I began mailing continually to that group, showing up at equestrian events, developed websites, and published a newsletter about commercial horse farms. Over time, I took over that market because I was the *specialist* who really understood the market.

After several years of selling these commercial horse farms, I was referred by one of my clients to list a very large Assisted Living Facility. Rather than refer the listing to another associate, I researched the Assisted Living marketplace and found that the most likely buyer would be one of the investor groups that owned other Assisted Living Facilities. I sent out flyers about the facility that I had listed to everyone who owned such a property in the tri-state area, and received enough inquiries that I sold the property very quickly. I then followed up with a "*sold*" flyer to the same group, stating that I still had buyers looking for similar facilities and to contact me if they were considering selling. I received 3 more listing calls on similar properties.

In order for farming to work, whether you're targeting a geographic area or targeting a type of property, you must be consistent in your message and you must be in front of the group regularly.

The most effective farming, like everything else, is face to face. If face to face is impractical, you can try mixing methods. Try interspersing phone calls to the farm and mailing the farm. Simply mailing to the group will take far longer to build any sort of relationship. Remember what we discussed earlier in this book about those individuals who open their mail over an open garbage can. You may never impact many of the people in your farm area simply by mailing.

One of the country's top sales trainers and an incredible motivational speaker, Tom Hopkins, was a master of farming. He would visit the same geographic area on a monthly basis, meeting each owner in person. His consistent effort to be in front of his farm area led him to be one of the top real estate professionals in the country.

One of the stories about Tom Hopkins that is most often repeated in real estate circles is how Tom hired neighborhood kids one year to help him deliver pumpkins to everyone in his farm area. He was so well remembered for the pumpkins that he put a picture of a pumpkin on his business card.

A Farming Story

I briefly met a very successful real estate agent several years ago who had been one of the top real estate agents in the world. When he began his career in the industry, he was working as a teacher and coach in a local high school. His income didn't pay all his bills, and he ended up sleeping on the gym floor because he didn't have an apartment.

Trying to earn extra money, he began a process of farming for business. He selected a geographic area and began knocking on doors every night until sundown. If I remember the story correctly, he went back to each house once a month in order to build rapport with the neighbors.

Within a few years, he was averaging 300 sales a year, and with an average sales price of around $125,000, he was earning well over a million dollars a year. Farming is a powerful technique. The problem is that too many agents give up on it before it begins to work. You should start seeing results within a year, but you need to stay at it consistently for at least 18 months before you can expect real results from it.

Farming Techniques

Farming can be one of the most effective prospecting methods over time. There are three keys to insure its effectiveness. The first key is to remember that you're in this for the long haul. I realize that I sound like a broken record, but I want to be clear. It may take you 12 months before you see your first lead or it may take 18 months. You cannot be discouraged, because your consistency and perseverance will eventually be rewarded with a strong relationship with your farm.

Secondly, your message must be consistent and regular. Farming will not work if you simply mail something to a group of houses 4 or 5 times a year. Typically for something like this to work, you need to contact the group at least once a month. During the first 90 days of any farming program, it's more effective to contact them every 2 weeks in order to build that name recognition that continues with a consistent message.

Third, and extremely important, is to vary the method of contact. For example, mailing to a group over and over and over again will probably generate some leads. To be truly effective, however, you should intersperse your farming with personal contact such as door knocking, community events or phone calls, and you should incorporate some sort of promotional item or give-away. Remember that most mail is simply thrown away. Until your geographic or demographic farm has met you and remembers you, most of the mailing is wasted.

Pumpkins and Flags

One of the greatest ideas I gleaned from Tom Hopkins was that any marketing should be fun. During his career in real estate, Tom got a bunch of neighborhood kids together in his farm area, purchased a truckload of pumpkins from a neighboring farm and delivered one to each home.

Because he was buying the pumpkins wholesale, he paid a fraction of what someone would pay at the store. Delivering something like a pumpkin sets you apart from every other Realtor who simply mails stuff to people.

The great thing about delivering pumpkins is that kids in the neighborhood see you coming and get excited. Everyone talks about what you're doing and neighbors come out and talk to you on a personal level, which is far different than a *salesperson* trying to get business.

My team and I tried the pumpkins our first year of farming. We found that too many of them broke and made a mess. Although I believe pumpkins are a great idea, we replaced pumpkins the next year with flags. Our marketing guru, Don, was able to secure a few hundred flags for us our first year, which grew to a few thousand over time.

We purchased large flags that were about 18" across the top, and stood about 2' off the ground, and because we purchased from the manufacturer, we have consistently paid less than 50 cents a piece year after year.

The key to the flag delivery was a little different than the pumpkin scenario. We selected certain neighborhoods that had many veterans. We then got a group together and delivered the flags from 8 pm until about 2 am. We pushed the flag poles into the ground close to the street in front of each home.

When the neighborhood woke up and went outside, they would see rows and rows of flags lining the street. At the bottom of each flag, we'd attach a card that said "Compliments of ..."

Although there would always be one or two people who would call and complain that we had trespassed on their property (the anti-American ones), we typically received several Thank You cards, personal notes and even a few cakes over the years. Many people really appreciated the effort.

Flags, however, do not replace that personal contact you get from door knocking. My suggestion is to send out an introductory letter to the neighborhood explaining you are the *"Neighborhood Professional"* or *"Neighborhood Realtor"* and include in your initial mailing a list of some of the homes recently sold in the neighborhood and their prices. Everyone likes to know what's going on in the neighborhood.

Follow up within 2 weeks by spending a weekend knocking on doors and introducing yourself. This is the hardest part of the process, but absolutely critical to building a strong, lifelong relationship with that community. Then you can follow up with mailings, sponsorship of a local event or local team, and some sort of special delivery item.

Demographic Farming

Remember that you can farm any demographic group or geographic area. The more creative you are in your selection of a target audience, the less likely you are to be in any serious competition with other agents.

As mentioned in earlier chapters, my team actively "farmed" horse properties. Agents across the country farm groups like attorneys, physicians, investors, stock brokers or any other potential target audience. When farming a demographic group, you have to determine first if it's a group that you can actually target, and second, lay out a game plan to do more than simply mail to them.

For example, attorneys are a great demographic group as a target market because they refer many clients to Realtors. However, you need to determine if you can effectively communicate with that group, and figure out a way to get in front of them. A game plan for farming attorneys will certainly include a regular mailing with a consistent message, but should also include personal contact. Three methods of direct contact with this demographic group are to cold call, to participate in industry events, and to sponsor programs for the group.

Getting Around the Gate Keeper

Cold calling attorneys is difficult, because most successful attorneys have receptionists and assistants trained to keep salespeople from talking to them. These individuals are known as "*gate keepers*". However, in the immortal words of legendary coach John Wooden, "*Don't let what you cannot do interfere with what you can do.*"

There are many techniques to getting yourself in front of attorneys and other individuals who employ these gate keepers. The good news is that if you employ some of these techniques, you will find very little competition for the business.

The receptionist or assistant is probably also the keeper of the attorney's schedule. One method is to let the receptionist or assistant know that you realize how important and how busy the attorney must be. You have a wonderful opportunity that you'd like to present to the attorney, and you'd like five minutes of the attorney's time. If the assistant can find a few meager minutes in the attorney's schedule for a venture that the attorney may find profitable, you promise that you will limit your conversation and introduction to five minutes. If you fail to live up to your promise, you will donate $100 to the charity of the attorney's choice in the attorney's name.

Remember not to be pushy. A pleasant demeanor goes a long way to getting in the door. This approach often surprises the gate keeper, catching them off-guard and may intrigue them enough to see what you really want.

Realtor: *"Hi, my name is Fred Dowling. I'm calling from Exceptional Realty Services and I'm hoping to speak with Attorney Seizholtsville."*

Receptionist: *"What is this regarding?"*

Realtor: *"I have a wonderful opportunity to present the attorney to help grow his business, and hopefully mine as well. Is there any chance he might be available?"*

Receptionist: *"I'm sorry, but Attorney Seizholtsville is a very busy person."*

Realtor: *"I understand that. I'm guessing you're also in charge of the attorney's schedule. I really am hoping to get a very short interview with him. I honestly only need 5 minutes of his time, and I'd love to meet him in person. Can I make a proposal?"*

Receptionist: *"I have another call. Can you please hold?"*

Realtor: *"Certainly."*

Soft music plays for three minutes and eight seconds.

Receptionist: *"I'm sorry. Mr. Dowling, was it?"*

Realtor: *"Yes. I was saying I really only need 5 minutes of the Attorney's time. Let me make a proposal. If you can find a few minutes to fit me into his schedule to meet with him in the next 2 weeks, I will absolutely limit our conversation to 5 minutes, which is 300 short seconds. If I go a second over 300, I will guarantee that I will donate $100 to your favorite charity in your name. Would you be able to find a few minutes for me?"*

Receptionist: *"Uh, can you run that by me again?"*

Realtor: *"Certainly. I'm not kidding when I say that I only need 5 minutes of the attorney's time. I will send you a written promise, by fax, that if you can get me into his schedule for a short 5 minutes, if I take a second over that amount of time, I will donate $100 in your name to the charity of your choice. Is there a charity you prefer?"*

You can be creative and come up with different approaches or methods to meet with attorneys. Certainly, you can also speak over the phone, but a face to face meeting is always the most powerful.

Once you've obtained an appointment to meet, prepare a package that outlines how you work and how you can assist the attorney's clients. In meeting with the attorney, pull out a watch so you can show the assistant that you are timing your meeting simply introduce yourself, and let the attorney know that you may be able to refer clients to the attorney, since you also deal with customers during crisis periods in their lives. You find it a pleasure meeting the attorney and would love to work with him or her.

Events and Sponsorships

Other methods to meet attorneys or any demographic group face to face include determining what events the demographic group participates in. Perhaps there is a local convention, meeting, or social event. Find a way to be part of the event or meeting. You may have to pay a fee or sponsorship in order to set up a stand or table. You may simply be able to show up and introduce yourself.

If you're targeting horse properties, make sure to set up a stand at local horse property events. If you're targeting NASCAR fans, then perhaps you can set up a stand at a NASCAR event, or hold a big tail-gate party. There are many ways to meet with demographic groups in person.

One creative method by an agent was to hold a free continuing educational workshop for attorneys. Title Insurance companies have ongoing workshops that count for continuing education for both attorneys and title agents. You may be able to split the cost of a speaker with a local title company and advertise to attorneys a free session that counts for CLE credits.

Farming Office Complexes

One of the most unique personal contact programs I've encountered I call 'office complex farming'. There are thousands of industrial parks and office parks around the country that have dozens of different businesses. Small manufacturing companies, insurance agencies and even dentists have offices in these multi-tenant office buildings and parks.

While most business owners will avoid meeting with salespeople who walk in off the street, the lynchpin of many organizations is the person at the front counter. This receptionist is often the conveyor of all information that goes into the office. The receptionist may also know exactly what's going on in everyone's lives in the company. Promotions, divorces, relocations and the selling of homes are all talked about over the water cooler in the front lobby of the office.

You may be able to turn this person into a bird dog for your business. The two great aspects of this technique are that you can do this kind of farming during the weekday, so you're not taking more time away from your family, and you can multiply your efforts by getting others to help refer you business and create a warm lead.

Rather than stopping at homes in a particular neighborhood where home owners may or may not be home, spend your day going through office buildings in the same area and meet the front desk person. Explain to them that you are the local Realtor and you're trying to grow your business. Does he or she know of anyone thinking about buying or selling real estate?

You may even bring a candy dish and fill it with chocolate or hard candy. I'm not suggesting doing anything expensive, but it gives you the ability to come back regularly, refill the candy dish and talk again with the receptionist.

Realtor: *"Wow, this is a nice looking office."* (You say while looking around the lobby – if it's true. If there are no redeeming qualities about the lobby, don't say it.) *"Hi, my name is Alex Cross. I'm a Realtor with Garden City Realtors around the corner from here. I'm just stopping by to introduce myself and hopefully grow my real estate business."*

Receptionist: *"Hello."*

Realtor: *"Is it okay if I leave some treats for your staff here on the counter?"*

Receptionist: *"I guess that's okay. Sure."*

- 184 -

Realtor: *"Who do you know in the office that might need the assistance of a good professional Realtor?"*

Receptionist: *"I can't think of anyone right now."*

Realtor: *"Okay, if someone mentions that they need some help, would you please have them call me? My card is right on the front of this dish."*

Receptionist: *"Okay."*

Remember that your initial conversation is only really to introduce yourself. Farming works by delivering a consistent repeated message. You will need to stop by the office at least monthly for the next year. You will discover, however, over time that you will become the confidant of many of the receptionists and you may be appreciated by staff members with "sweet tooths."

Corporate Farming

In keeping with the theme of multiplying your efforts, other great farming targets are those people in positions of power who relocate people in and out of your area. Personnel directors or relocation directors or human resource managers may be in charge of hiring and firing at a company.

Unfortunately, as we discussed earlier with attorneys, many of these individuals are protected from salespeople by their own receptionists or gate keepers. You may have to find a way around the gate keeper in order to speak directly and regularly with these people. The benefit is that a company relocating 5 or 6 people in or out of an area in a given year generates 5 or 6 buyers or sellers for you regularly.

Mail hardly ever works to generate leads from these managers because they simply receive too much mail each day. You need to find a way to meet with them in person.

As I suggested with prospecting for attorney business, offer the receptionist or gate keeper something of value in return for scheduling five minutes or less with the relocation director or human resources director so that you may introduce yourself. The technique listed earlier for offering to donate money to his or her favorite charity has worked well for our team.

Relocation Companies

Some corporations are already signed up with relocation companies, such as Cartus or Prudential. These firms manage the moves of employees around the country or around the world, and assign the listing and buyer leads out to agents in their networks.

Relocation companies or mobility companies are very difficult to land as clients because they only want the best in any particular area or region. You may, however, build a relationship with them over time, as you would with any organization and eventually earn the opportunity to make a presentation of your marketing and service program.

Years ago, one of our target companies was Home Equity, which eventually merged with Cartus. Home Equity had a relocation contact with "M", the large player in our marketplace that I wrote about early in the book. At the time, we had about twenty agents and M had around 400. We believed it be nearly impossible to unseat them as the relocation center at the time.

Diligently, we called the director of the Pennsylvania region and asked for an application. The director's assistant explained that she was very busy and couldn't speak with us. However, we did learn that every area had a primary real estate company and a secondary or associate company which received a far smaller percentage of the leads. This was designed in case there was an issue or conflict with the first company. Home Equity already had a primary and an associate in our area, but the director's assistant still provided us with an application to fill out.

A little research allowed us to find out information about the relocation director, including her birthday. For her birthday, we sent her a huge bouquet of flowers and balloons. Yes, it was an obvious attempt to buy business, but it also was outside the scope of what anyone else had tried. It stood out as unique.

When contracts came up to be renegotiated, we were allowed the opportunity to compete and we won the contract. I don't believe we even would have had the possibility of truly competing for that spot had we not maintained consistent contact and done something outrageous.

Networking Organizations

When you first enter the field of real estate, you typically have more time than money. Use that time wisely, and get yourself in front of as many decision makers as possible.

Join any local community groups that make sense. Go to the local Chamber of Commerce Meetings and local planning meetings.

Another good source of leads for our associates has been to join networking or business builder groups, like LeTip. LeTip is a national organization with local chapters. Each chapter only allows one person in from each business category. For example, there can only be one chiropractor, one heating and air conditioning vendor and one payroll specialist. The group tries to grow each others businesses, and presses each member to "tip" the other members with possible leads. These types of groups can help multiply your efforts to get your name out in front of potential clients. Additionally, each person in a LeTip group is probably a decision maker in a business, and these may be potential buyers and sellers for you in time.

Other Networking

There are many other professions that are closely tied to real estate. My team receives regular referrals from local attorneys because they often speak with clients about their needs before the client contacts a realtor. Mortgage brokers, bank lending departments, and architects can be good sources of leads. For commercial Realtors or investment specialists, commercial lenders, geologists, engineers, surveyors, zoning officers and even financial planners are all great sources of leads.

Summary

When starting your career in real estate, you need to spend a significant part of your time proactively prospecting for business using short term methods. If you don't develop a plan for short term prospecting, you will most likely fail in your career because you won't last long enough to earn a significant living.

However, long term business growth allows the real estate business to become "fun" for agents and brokers. Long term growth comes as a result of both delivering exceptional service to your clients, and developing long term prospecting targets.

Rather than cold calling for the rest of your career, you may make contact with a few attorneys who each provide you a dozen good leads for listings each year. You may sign a relocation contract which leads to another five to ten sales each year. Your contact with your past clients and sphere of influence may deliver another ten or twenty transactions each year.

Long term methods will keep you in business, earning a great living, for as long as you choose. A mixture of long term and short term methods are best when building a real estate career for life.

Chapter 9: Using Guarantees

Samuel Johnson: "Nothing will ever be attempted if all possible objections must first be overcome."

Spend a few days simply talking to friends and relatives who have sold a home at some point in their lives. Did they have any challenges or problems when selling? Would they experience something differently the next time? What was the most frustrating part of selling a property?

I've spoken with hundreds of home sellers about this issue, and there are several primary complaints that are repeated by nearly every unhappy seller. Of course, some are unhappy with the sales price they received, and although they often blame the agent, that is not something typically in the control of Realtors. The primary complaints that are in our control all have to do with maintaining contact with the seller throughout the process of selling the property.

The most common responses we heard from our research were:

- The Realtor never advertised the home.
- The Realtor rarely advertised or marketed the home.
- The Realtor was unresponsive or didn't call back when the owner called them.

- The Realtor didn't maintain any sort of regular contact and the owner felt like they had to chase the Realtor in order to get feedback on showings.

With regard to the advertising complaints, when we went back to determine whether or not the properties were actually advertised, in most cases, we found that they were. The problem was that the agent never communicated to the client that the property was being advertised. Sending out a copy of the ad or calling and telling the owner where and when the property was being marketed would have led to less frustration on the owner's part.

Most of the complaints about Realtors revolve around the agent's contact with the client. Keeping in touch and sending out copies of ads may also have allowed the agent to re-list the property if it were expiring or perhaps reduce the property price to a saleable level.

If you, as a Realtor, set a specific time each week to keep in touch with your current customers, you're far more likely to get the property sold, and you're also far more likely to garner referrals. You need to show your clients what you're doing each step of the way.

Lowering the Barrier of Resistance

Property owners who have had a poor experience before, or who have been warned about bad experiences from friends, relatives or co-workers, will be hesitant about signing an exclusive real estate listing without some assurance that they will get service.

They don't want to be stuck with a poor or unresponsive agent. This is one of the primary reasons some owners decide to try *"For Sale by Owner"*. They at least feel in control of the selling situation. It is also the reason many sellers are hesitant to sign lengthy listing contracts with an agent they just met. They don't *really* know how you're going to treat them after signing the contract to list.

Guarantees are a written method of lowering the barrier of resistance to the owner signing a contract with you. *"If you are unhappy with my service, I will cancel this listing without any penalty"* is an absolutely strong indication that you believe in your ability to sell the property and you believe in your service.

"If I don't return a call to you within 24 hours, I will donate $100 to the charity of your choice" is another strong promise that gives the prospect a feeling that you really will do what you say you're going to do. And truthfully, you will work harder to make sure you don't fall short of your guarantees.

When making an offer of any guarantee, make sure it's something you can live up to. If you promise the moon, the stars and the ocean, and you only deliver the moon, clients will be very disappointed and will not refer you. If you promise the moon and at least deliver the moon and the stars, they will enthusiastically refer you to their friends and relatives.

The Listing Cancellation Guarantee

Several of you, dear readers, have flipped to this page and are now shouting that I have completely lost my mind. *"Give home sellers the option to cancel their listing?"* you ask. *"They'll all be cancelling two weeks after I start marketing the home. Every home seller becomes frustrated because the home isn't selling quickly enough."*

It is true that selling a home is one of the most stressful times in a person's life. It is also true that if the home isn't selling, the seller often blames the real estate agent or their marketing. So why should you consider making such an offer?

Remember that one of your goals is to offer a unique service or unique selling proposition that will entice a client to call you. Another goal is to lower the barrier of resistance to entice the customer to work with you exclusively.

One of the seller's primary fears in selling their property is to entrust their most valuable asset to someone they may just be meeting for the first time. The most powerful way to reduce that fear is to show the client that you are *so* certain of your level of service and commitment to their cause that you're willing to allow them to cancel their listing contract if they are dissatisfied with your service.

There are agents across the country offering this guarantee under a variety of titles, such as:

- The Listing Service Guarantee
- The Listing Cancellation Guarantee
- The Easy Exit Guarantee
- The Listing Exit Guarantee
- And many others.

The question many of you are forming is *"Will some of my listings use this clause to cancel their listings after I've put my time and money into marketing and servicing their property?"* The honest answer is *"Yes".* Some *will* cancel their listings. Some of these sellers may even use this clause in order to cancel the listing and try to sell the home directly to a friend or co-worker who became interested in the home after it was listed.

Again, yes, you may lose some money on some listings. However, you'll find that by offering this guarantee, you'll be likely to take more listings and those additional listings will generate additional buyers for you.

You will also find that you'll become a better agent because you'll have to improve your service and regularly maintain contact with your clients in order to avoid their cancellation of your listing.

Typically, this guarantee will give you a Net Gain in listings, sales and generated business.

Because this guarantee or technique involves releasing a client from a contract, before using this system, you must speak with your broker or manager and obtain their permission to use it. Listings typically belong to the company, not the individual agent, so you must have that authorization.

Call-Back Guarantee

Over the past two decades, I have personally listed hundreds of homes that expired off the market with other Realtors. One of the most common complaints I've heard from these home sellers is: *"I listed my home with Joe Agent and I never heard from him again. When I called Joe, he didn't even bother to call me back."*

Home sellers anecdotally tell these stories to each other. This problem alone is probably one of the primary factors helping to form the low opinions many consumers hold of the entire real estate industry.

To overcome this concern, or to turn this potential negative into a positive, you can provide the potential client with a guarantee that you will call them regularly and you will return their call promptly.

This guarantee can be accomplished in many different ways, but you must carefully choose what you absolutely *can* do in order for this guarantee to work. Remember that making a commitment you cannot fulfill is far worse than making no commitment in the first place.

For example, some of you may be able to commit to returning a call within 4 hours if your schedule permits that. Perhaps you're a very busy Realtor and don't know if you can return calls in between appointments. You may want to guarantee that you'll call each listing every single week with feedback on showings and updates, and you'll return any call made by your client within 24 hours or by the end of the day.

Any commitment like this that you advertise should also include a penalty if you are unable to perform. For example, if you promise to call back within 24 hours and you don't, you may want to donate $100 to the seller's favorite charity. Maybe instead, you want to take $50 off the seller's costs at settlement for each infraction.

The promise has to be believable, and the consequences have to be something that dramatically shows the client that you keep your promises.

Example:

"Judy's Update Guarantee – I will call you with feedback and updates every single week on Thursday afternoon. If I fail to call you, I promise to give you $100 back on your commission at settlement."

Marketing Guarantees

If you are planning to use marketing guarantees, make sure you deliver what you offer the client. Advertising and marketing guarantees are not hard to fulfill if you work diligently.

Some popular marketing guarantees include:

- *"Your home will be advertised on 99 sites on the Internet"* – Trust me, if you look, you will find plenty of places online to advertise your listings.

- *"My team will use 8 different advertising methods to get your property sold"* – If you think about it, there are plenty of different venues for marketing and advertising your listings. The MLS, Newspaper, Homes Magazines, Internet, Flyers, Signage, Open Houses and brochure boxes are all great methods of advertising.

- *"We insure your home sale with our 57 point marketing program"* – Create a list of every single thing you do to market a home. If your office does caravans of new listings, include it as a point in your marketing system. List everything out and count up the number.

- *"I will advertise your home every day until it sells"*. This sounds great, but is honestly easy to fulfill. The home is on the MLS every single day. It's also on the Internet every day, and there's a sign in the yard every day. This tag line can also be used as a USP.

Buyer's Guarantee – Sell it Free

If you've been selling real estate for any period of time, you will inevitably run into cases of buyer's remorse. Buyer's remorse is when a buyer, after making an offer, decides the home they are buying is priced too high, their offer was too high, the neighborhood is wrong, there are hidden defects and the house is too small.

Buying a home is one of the most stressful times in a person's life and it's only natural to second guess a big decision. Unfortunately, buyer's remorse leads to arguments, resentment and some buyer's pulling all sorts of tricks to get back out of their commitment to purchase a particular home.

One guarantee that helps put buyers at ease is to make the offer that if they are unhappy with their purchase any time in the first year, you will resell the home for free. In other words, you will not charge any listing commission on the sale of the home if they decide to resell the home in one year.

As with any guarantee, if you have to "pay off" and sell a home without a commission, you may be carrying some costs of advertising. However, the number of buyers who are unhappy and resell within a year of moving into a home is so small, the positives of this approach will outweigh the negatives of some unpaid advertising expense.

Outrageous guarantees

Remember that the fundamental purpose of prospecting is to entice a potential client into raising their hand and identifying themselves as someone looking to buy or sell real estate.

Some real estate agents use offers so outrageous that buyers and sellers simply *need* to find out how the agent can make such a claim. The emotional pull of the offer is irresistible.

Outrageous offers include *"If I can't sell your home, I'll buy it"*, *"If I can't sell your home in XX days, I'll pay you $10,000 cash"* and *"If you're unhappy with your home after buying it, I'll buy it back from you."*

Obviously a Realtor can't make money if he or she is buying their own listings at market value. The closing costs to buy and sell each home would eat them alive. Just as obvious is the fact that a real estate agent or broker can't simply promise to pay a home seller $10,000 cash if the agent is unable to sell their home in only 60 days. This is especially true in areas of the country where the average home sale is taking 90 to 120 days.

Home sellers, however, always hold out hope that some agent, somewhere, has a secret that will sell their home painlessly and instantly and for a price much higher than they've been told by the last three Realtors. Buyers and sellers can believe the most outrageous lies if they're beneficial to the buyer or seller.

For example, a few years ago, I was competing for a listing in a neighborhood made up primarily of new construction. The home I was evaluating was directly across from the model home and the exact same model as the model home. I explained to the home owner that he was very likely to get the same price as the model. He informed me that the agent who preceded me explained he could sell for $100,000 more than the model.

"How is that possible?" I asked the home owner. *"Simple,"* he replied, *"the other agent markets to New Jersey buyers moving into the area, and they pay more for homes."* As a Realtor, you may laugh, but the truth is that the home owner bought that story hook, line and sinker because it made the home owner believe he could get more for his home.

Although I felt the other agent was not working in the home owner's best interest, and probably inflating the list price in order to get a For Sale sign up and attract buyers, he got the listing. The moral of the story is that our customers hear what they want to hear.

So, you may ask, how do agents and brokers make such outrageous claims as offering $10,000 cash if the home isn't sold in 53 days and 8 minutes? By setting the bar too high for the client to actually participate in the program, or by offering a trade where the agent still earns their fee.

Please let me stress that these offers are not for the faint-of-heart. As I said earlier, there is a fine line between marketing to entice clients to make contact with you, and doing clients a disservice. Your intent, at the very least, should be to truly assist your clients in doing what is in their best interests.

We'll Buy Your Home – Fair Trade

This can be done in two ways. Remember that buying a home is generally a losing proposition for a Realtor or a real estate firm, but can be a significant benefit to a home seller who needs to be certain the home will sell in order to make their move.

Although many variations of this program exist, the typical "Fair Trade" version of this program has three basic requirements. First, the home has to be on the market for a reasonable amount of time at a reasonable price in order to give the home a fair chance of selling.

To estimate a reasonable period of time for marketing, a broker will typically set the time frame at 50% higher than the average time to sell a similar home. For example, if the average home of this type is selling in 60 days in the local market, the broker will generally offer to buy the home 90 days after the beginning of the listing. In order to insure the home is marketed at a reasonable price, this approach generally requires the home owner to have an independent appraisal to be done and the price to be set within a predetermined range of the appraisal. If the home appraises for $200,000, the agreement may be that the home must be listed within 1% or 2% of that $200,000 and any offer received within 5% of the listing price is considered sold so that the broker doesn't have to purchase the home.

Secondly, in most cases, this program requires the home owner to purchase their next home through the broker, meaning the broker at least receives a commission on the buying end of the transaction.

In order to insure the broker doesn't lose money, additional caveats to the contract might be employed. One common addition is that the broker does not buy the home at full price, but rather purchases the home at some preconceived discount.

Another variation is that the home seller must reduce the price a predetermined amount at certain intervals, such as every 10 days or every two weeks until the buyout occurs. Again, these help to get the home sold prior to any buyout. An alternative might be that the property owner pays additional fees at settlement for the buyout.

None of these conditions of a buyout program are created to injure the home owner. The goal truly is to get the property listed and get the home owner where they need to go in time. However, the broker does not want to lose money in the process.

We'll Buy Your Home – Outrageous Ad

In some parts of the country, where homes are taking many months to sell, agents are advertising they will buy the home in just weeks or a few months for cash if the home is unsold. In these cases, the agent is typically advertising to get in the door.

I am not suggesting this strategy is a good strategy or a bad strategy. I personally do not employ outrageous advertising because I have a difficult time beginning a relationship with a client by using misleading statements or marketing.

However, a successful Realtor should be familiar with all the various forms of marketing that attract clients, and the decision whether or not to use a particular type of marketing should be up to the agent and their broker.

Again, when a Realtor advertises that they will buy the client's home if unsold in a certain period of time, the Realtor is setting the bar for actually purchasing the home so high that the home owner typically will not take the deal. Either the offer to purchase is at a wholesale price which is far below what the typical home seller is willing to take, or the criteria for participating in the program is difficult for the home owner to accept.

For example, an ad that advertises the Realtor will purchase the home in only 60 days might have the following restrictions:

1. There must be at least 3 other homes in the neighborhood of similar size that have also sold in 60 days or less within the past 6 months.
2. The home must be appraised and the list price set within 2% of the appraised price of the home. The 60 day buyout time clock doesn't start until the appraisal is completed and the price is set.
3. The home must be professionally staged and home inspected. The home owner must make any repairs found by the home inspector and stage the home per the stager. The 60 day buy-out time clock doesn't start until these items are completed.

These restrictions may surprise the home owner. The agent simply explains that buying homes at market price is a losing proposition for a Realtor. A Realtor simply can't buy a home and resell it to recoup their out of pocket cost. In order to offer such a great program and really put so much of the agent's money at stake, the owner has to be willing to do what it takes to get the home sold in a reasonable time frame.

Most home owners will say *"I'm not willing to pay for an appraisal, home inspection and home staging expert in order to participate in this program."* The response by the Realtor is, *"That's no problem. I can still list your home for sale, and I can still put my exceptional marketing program to work selling your home."*

The outrageous guarantee has worked to get the Realtor in the door to meet with the client and lay out a marketing plan.

Cash Offer Guarantee

"If your home isn't sold in 37.5 days, I'll pay you $5200 in cash." This guarantee program has been done in several different ways as well.

The "Fair Trade" method is simply to offer the home owner a cash rebate of a portion of the commission at settlement if the home isn't sold in the average time frame of the market. This method impresses many home sellers because you, the Realtor, are so certain of your marketing ability that you gamble the home will be sold.

Like the listing cancellation guarantee, you may lose some money by making this offer. You may discount your services in some cases by offering cash back if the home isn't sold. What you have to determine, through trial and error, is how many more listings will you obtain by making the offer versus how much money you'll lose as homes don't sell in the time.

The outrageous cash offer will state an artificially low time frame to sell or a high cash reward if the home isn't sold. Home owners are attracted because they believe the ad means the agent will really only take a certain number of days to sell the home.

Like the "we'll buy your home" ad, this offer usually comes with pretty stringent requirements on the part of the home owner. This program may also require an appraisal, home inspection and a maximum listing price versus the appraisal.

Buyers - We'll Buy Your Home Back

A variation on the "Sell the home for free" guarantee outlined earlier in this chapter, this is a guarantee made by the Realtor to buy back the home if the buyer is unhappy with their purchase.

As with any outrageous guarantee, there are typically caveats. One condition may be that the buyer attempt to sell the home at the appraised value for some period of time, and the home is considered sold if an offer within 5% of the list price is received. Another condition may be that the Realtor will buy back the home at a wholesale price.

Summary

Remember that guarantees serve two purposes: first, you want to find ways to attract clients to speak with you about your services. Second, you want to lower the barrier of resistance for a client to sign a contract with you.

The key with making any guarantee is that you must live up to the level of service you offer. If you fall short of what you offer, you are unlikely to ever receive a referral from the client.

Chapter 10 – Putting it Together

When executed correctly, a strong prospecting program with a strong follow-up and service program will slingshot your career into high gear. One of the primary reasons most real estate agents fail is that they don't begin a prospecting program when they begin their career.

As I wrote in the first chapter, there are four components to a successful prospecting system:

1.   Select Your Target Market

2.   Select Your Method of Contact

3.   Give Your Prospect Something of Value

4.   Follow Up Consistently

When agents begin their careers with my firm in Pennsylvania, I beg them to take their careers seriously. Consider it a full time job, but instead of having someone telling you what to do all day long, you must structure your own time and lay out your own plan of attack.

Unfortunately, most agents entering the field of real estate fail. They fail because they don't take the time to plan their career and develop it. You don't have to be a statistic.

At the end of this chapter are two sample prospecting plans. The first is for elder clients who are downsizing or going into assisted living. The second is for vacant lot owners. These are simply examples to follow.

As the saying goes, an elephant can be eaten if it's done one bite at a time. Schedule time over the next week to simply select and target market and then, using examples in this book, begin building a plan of attack.

Next, start executing the plan of attack. Too many people are paralyzed by not having every duck in a row. You may not yet have a website designed to target your market. You may not have a great brochure done yet. It doesn't matter. You need to start prospecting. Do what you can in a short time period and plan for the rest, but don't hesitate to act because everything isn't quite perfected yet.

Once again, the two fundamental truths about prospecting are that you *must* prospect consistently in order to be successful, and you *must* realize that prospecting is a process, not an event. Plan, execute your plan and then step back to analyze what worked and what didn't. Plan again and execute again.

As with anything in life, your career is ultimately up to you. You can choose to fail or you can choose to succeed. I hope you choose to be the best that you possibly can be!

Plan A: Long Term Prospecting of Empty Nesters

In the first 10 Days

❑ Compile or purchase a mailing list of seniors over 65 years old who own a home in my target market area.
❑ Add the mailing list to my database with the contact type of "Senior"
❑ Write your first mailing to this group.
❑ Plan to take a senior designation from the National Association of Realtors.
❑ Determine what kind of guarantees you'll offer seniors to lower the barrier of resistance to their using your services.

In the first 30 Days

❑ Send out initial mailing to the group announcing that you are the senior specialist and can assist them with their needs.
❑ Begin sending 5 hand written notes per day to this group.
❑ Contact elder care attorneys and assisted living facilities to see if you can network with them or trade referrals.
❑ Write an informational brochure *"The 9 Grave Mistakes Made by Seniors Moving from their Homes and How to Avoid Them."*
❑ Send out second mailing within the first 30 days for maximum impact, and include a method for seniors to obtain a copy of your free report.

In the first 90 Days

❑ Plan to set up a booth at a SeniorFest or other senior event.

- ❏ Set up a website dedicated to helping seniors to facilitate their moves, giving away free information.
- ❏ Advertise your informational brochure and your web site with free information in any senior magazines or newsletters.

Plan B: Long Term Prospecting of Vacant Lot Owners

In the first 10 Days

❑ Compile or purchase a mailing list of vacant lots in my target market area.
❑ Add the mailing list to my database with the contact type of "Vacant Lot Owners"
❑ Write your first mailing to this group.
❑ Talk to local zoning office, planning commission or office for building permits and determine what steps need to be taken in order to erect a home on a vacant lot.
❑ Determine what kind of guarantees you'll offer land owners to lower the barrier of resistance to their using your services.

In the first 30 Days

❑ Send out initial mailing to the group announcing that you are the lot and land specialist and can assist them with their needs.
❑ Begin sending 5 hand written notes per day to this group.
❑ Write an informational brochure *"The 9 Mistakes Made by Vacant Lot Owners that could bury them and How to Avoid Them."*
❑ Send out second mailing within the first 30 days for maximum impact, and include a method for lot owners to obtain a copy of your free report.

In the first 90 Days

❑ Begin calling builders to determine if they are in need of building lots to create a built-in buying group for the vacant land.

☐ Set up a website dedicated to helping land owners to facilitate their sales, giving away free information. Include a list of lots available.

☐ Advertise your informational brochure and your web site with free information in any magazines or newsletters that make sense for this target group.

Other Books by Loren Keim
Order online at www.RealEstatesNextLevel.com

How to Sell Your Home in Any Market: 6 Reasons Why Your Home Isn't Selling... and What You Can Do to Fix Them. (2008 – Sourcebooks)

People sell homes every year in every market throughout the country. However as the market slows down, an owner must compete for fewer buyers in the marketplace. And even when the market is hot, there are still always homes that just don't sell.

The primary reasons why houses don't sell include poor staging, improper pricing, incorrect marketing, functional obsolescence and location challenges (or that people just aren't buying in the area!)

This easy-to-read, well-organized book explains how to fix your house and your sales technique to sell your home faster and for top dollar.

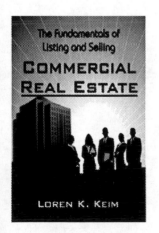

The Fundamentals of Listing and Selling Commercial Real Estate

A complete foundation for a career in the Commercial Real Estate Industry, the text contains a comprehensive study of property and investment analysis, mortgages and leases, as well as practice techniques such as prospecting, presentations, and negotiating.

Index

A

Absentee Owners, 29
ACT, 82
Action Plan, 91
Answering Machines, 119
Arthur Brisbane, 21
Attorney Referrals, 31
Attraction Techniques, 55, 62
Automatic Listing Updates, 70

B

Bank Foreclosures, 26
Booths at Events, 45
Builders, 30
Business Brokerage, 34
Buyer's Guarantee
    Sell the Home for Free, 198

C

Call Back Guarantee, 195
Cartus, 31, 186
Century 21 Keim, 134
Chamber of Commerce, 187
Christopher Reeves, 41
Client Gatherings, 43, 111
Cold Call
    Elements, 115
Cold Calling, 114
    Creative, 118
    For Buyers, 117
Commercial Real Estate
    Prospecting, 33
Contact Management Program, 82
Corporate Farming, 185

D

Database, 82
    Building, 129

Demographic Farming, 179
Demographic Groups, 31
Dennis Waitley, 113
Direct Response Marketing, 19
Door Hangers, 125
Door Knocking, 42, 121, 122
Door Knocking System
    3 Step Process, 127
Drip Systems, 84

E

Elbert Hubbard, 81
E-mail, 54
Emmitt Smith, 59
Emotional Response, 50
Employee Relocation Council, 31
Empty Nesters, 209, 211
E-Newsletters, 86
equestrian properties, 14
Events, 182
Evidence of Success, 53, 88
Expired Listings, 27, 131
    Expired Packages, 141
    Felt Tip Card System, 147
    Morning Delivery System, 143
    Scripts, 136
    Seller's Perspective, 132

F

Farming, 173
    Demographic, 179
    Office Complexes, 183
    Techniques, 176
First Time Buyers, 28
Floyd Wickman, 133, 149
Follow Up Systems, 20
Follow-Up Systems, 81
For Sale By Owners, 27, 154
For Sale By Owners'
    Reasons for Failure, 155
Foreclosed Properties, 29

Free Reports, 65, 68
FSBO - I have a buyer approach,
  164
FSBO - Mortgage Approach, 166
FSBO - Relocation Approach, 158
FSBO Survival Pack, 168

G

Gate Keeper, 179
Geographic Farming, 30
George Eliot, 41
Gerry Ballinger, 59, 60
Gooder Group, 86
Green Homes, 32
Guarantee
  Cash Offer, 204

H

historic homes, 14
Historic Homes, 13, 32
Horse Property, 32
Hospitality Properties, 33
Humor, 93
Humorous Cards, 52

I

Indirect Meetings, 44
Internet Leads, 34
Investment Property, 30
iPhone, 77

J

Jay Abraham, 60
Jim Droz, 175
Joe Stumpf, 60
Just Listed, 50
Just Sold, 50
Just Sold Prospecting, 28

K

Kevin W. McCarthy, 113

L

Lending Tree, 34
LeTip, 188
Le-Tip, 89
Letters VS Postcards, 48
Life Events, 28
Listing Video, 78
Long Term Marketing, 16
Long Term Prospecting
  Markets, 29
    Understanding Numbers, 36
Long Term Prospecting Methods,
  99
Lowering the Barrier of Resistance,
  192

M

Mailers, 47
Market Evaluations, 69
Marketing Warfare, 13
mean people, 122
Method of Contact, 12, 15, 207
Methods of Contact, 41
Mike Ferry, 133

N

Networking Organizations, 187
New Construction, 30
Newsletters, 53, 85
Newsworthy Marketing, 64
Niche Market, 74

O

Office Buildings, 33
Online Strategy, 91
Open House Prospecting, 28
Outrageous guarantees, 199

P

Performance Guarantee, 75
Personal Contact

Methods, 41
personal notes, 105
Personal notes, 105
Personnel Departments, 31
Phone Contacts
    Methods, 46
Pre-foreclosure Properties, 29

Projected Income Chart, 40
Projecting Your Income, 38
Promotional Items, 95
Prudential, 31

R

Reactive Prospecting, 15
Recipe Cards, 52
Redevelopment Opportunities, 33
Relocation Companies, 186
REO Companies, 30
Retail Properties, 33

S

Senior Communities, 32
Short Term Prospecting, 16, 18,
    113
    Markets, 27
    Other Methods, 172
    Understanding Numbers, 34
Special Delivery, 54
Sphere of Influence, 18, 29, 107
Sphere of Influence Prospecting,
    100
Stephen King, 22

T

Target Market, 12
Target Markets, 23
Testimonial Letters, 87
Testimonials, 53
Third Party Relocation Companies,
    31
Tom Hopkins, 174, 175, 177
Top Producer, 91, 134
Top Producer Software, 82, 92
Trade Shows, 45

U

Unique Selling Proposition, 73, 74
Unique Service, 74
Update Guarantee, 197

V

Vacant Land Parcels, 30
Vacant Property Owners, 130
Value Added Prospecting, 19
Video, 78
Viral Marketing, 76

W

Wayne Gretzky, 23
Workshops, 42

Y

YouTube, 77